# The Seasoned Soul

# The Seasoned Soul

## Reflections on Growing Older

ELIZA BLANCHARD

Skinner House Books
BOSTON

www.skinnerhouse.org

Printed in the United States

Cover design by Kathryn Sky-Peck
Text design by Jeff Miller

print ISBN: 978-1-55896-662-8
eBook ISBN: 978-1-55896-663-5

6 5 4 3 2
15 14 13 12

We gratefully acknowledge permission from Deborah Raible to reprint "We build on foundations we did not lay . . ." by Peter Raible; and from Rebecca Parker to reprint "There is a love holding me . . ." by Rebecca Parker.

Library of Congress Cataloging-in-Publication Data
Blanchard, Eliza, 1950–
    The seasoned soul : reflections on growing older / Eliza Blanchard.
        p. cm.
    ISBN 978-1-55896-662-8 (pbk. : alk. paper) — ISBN 978-1-55896-663-5
(ebook)
    1. Aging—Religious aspects—Meditations. 2. Older people—Prayers and devotions. I. Title.
    BL625.4.B63 2012
    204'.40846—dc23
                                                            2011043085

# Contents

*Dear Reader,*

The comedian George Carlin joked that only children get excited about growing older. Once we're adults, we seem to forget our wonder at the changes and new skills that aging can bring. This loss of our sense of awe and expectation—as well as the daily challenges of growing older—can weigh heavily on our spirits.

I wrote this book because I felt an increasing need for a manual to help rekindle my own sense of wonder and the possibility of some kind of achievement. I began by gathering wisdom, much of it from elders. And I looked for inspiration from many cultures and religious traditions, since growing older is a journey we all share. The reflections that came out of this process will, I hope, help to lift your heart and grow your spirit. They include universal themes, such as how to love, bear pain, grieve, deepen relationships and create new ones, retain dignity and passion, serve others, change, and deal with fear. These are some of the challenges we all face as we grow older; the good news is that we have more experience, compassion, and understanding to bring to them. The reflections in this book are designed to help you tap into your resources, lightening your spirits as well as the spirits of those around you. They may be read in any order, for reflection, journaling, a *lectio divina* spiritual practice, or sharing with a loved one. They can also be used in group settings. For example, they can serve as a basis for small group discussions, or enhance a workshop on ageing and sageing.

Sound and healthy spirits help us live with greater joy, intention, and appreciation. I hope this book kindles a flame that lights your spirit's journey.

*Blessings,*
*Eliza Blanchard*

# With a Beginner's Mind

Youth is a gift of nature. Aging is a work of art.

—Anonymous

Most of us realize that our lives are gifts, and sometimes—in spite of dental appointments and lost car keys—we remember to feel gratitude. Some of us make the time to express our appreciation on a regular basis, grounding ourselves in the reminder of all that we have.

From the vantage point of adulthood, we may newly appreciate how our childhoods, even our teenage years, were like presents, unearned and unexpected. The gifts of health, energy, and delight in the unfolding world came simply wrapped. Most of us don't recall unwrapping them—we just rolled out of bed each day, went to school, learned to play baseball or to jump rope with our friends, did our homework (sometimes), and fell asleep easily. These are gifts only a mother as generous as Nature could give.

In our middle years, we begin to notice our elders reporting aches and pains, encountering limitations, or experiencing other difficulties. We begin to see our own futures. When we face something new or difficult for the first time, we often call on experts. We might read books, consult the Internet, take classes, or talk to others who have more experience. We can glean certain techniques, adopting ideas that work for us and rejecting those that don't. We might then adapt or even invent approaches as we go.

But this is technique. If aging is an art, then artistry grows from a passion for expressing ourselves. Our passion flows from thankfulness for the ever-shifting and transforming gift of life. By observing, practicing, adapting, and creating responses to the happenings of our lives, we mature, becoming time's artisans. True artists improvise, using materials and inspiration available to them, staying open to what comes their way and letting inspiration animate their vision.

With beginner's minds and youthful curiosity, with hard-won wisdom and resourcefulness, we can all become the artists of our lives.

# Becoming Miz Kate

Kate Winston [was] a warm, kind church woman
who visited my hometown in the summers and
spoiled me with fancy clothes and attention.

— MARIAN WRIGHT EDELMAN

Hopefully we all had at least one older person in our young
lives—a mentor, a guardian angel, an aunt or uncle or a
neighbor who acted like one. Marian Wright Edelman dedi-
cates her book *Lanterns* to three such women, including "Miz
Kate," as this well-brought-up Southern child called her.

Though this description of her is brief, we can imagine
Miz Kate, or someone like her, very easily. A woman late in
middle age, maybe widowed, maybe not; maybe childless,
maybe not. A Christian woman, in that she believes in emu-
lating the warm welcome of Jesus. Someone who values
community and invests herself in it.

Not only is Miz Kate kind but she notices things—like
a respectful young girl's love of books and of space where
she can think to herself in peace and quiet. Miz Kate cares
enough to spend time and thought on a young person, and
always maintains her generous spirit. In fact, Marian Wright

Edelman grows up to become a powerful advocate for children and families partly because of Miz Kate's example.

What a gift to have a mentor! Mentors shaped Edelman's life in unexpected and unforgettable ways. And what a gift to be able to mentor a young person. Miz Kate surely enjoyed delighting her protégé with special clothes—but in Edelman's brief recollection, we sense that Edelman experienced the elder's attention as the true gift.

For as much as we gain experience and wisdom as we grow, perhaps the most important quality we gain is empathy. Like Miz Kate, we enrich our own lives along with others' when we take the time to notice how much *attending to* is a treasured kind of ministry.

Miz Kate didn't need to spend every moment of every day with Edelman to make a difference in her life. But she did need to be fully present during their time together. A child's radar is finely tuned to the authentic—what matters most to them is our honesty with them and with ourselves.

To become mentors, we must genuinely care. We must show up, and give young people our full attention. And sometimes a little spoiling is precisely what's needed.

# A Guide for the Journey

When you are old, when you are approaching the
end of life's journey, it would seem to be the most
natural thing to talk of death. If the family is going
abroad for the summer, especially if it's for the first
time, conversation for months ahead is taken up
with places to visit, preparations for the journey,
friends or relatives to be greeted.

— JOHN LaFARGE

How ironic! Faced with the most intriguing destination of
all, many of us live in denial about where we're going and
how best to get there. Planning any other trip, we eagerly talk
with others and consult guides and maps. We prepare docu-
ments and anticipate expenses. We pack what we'll need. We
look forward to meeting people along the way, and to all we'd
like to see and do as we journey.

But the thought of a one-way ticket scares the daylights
out of many of us. Some of us refuse to think about the trip
and stay stuck at home. Others treat the journey toward the
end of life like a road trip — grab some beers, some music and
fun folks, travel whatever highway, and when the road runs
out, it runs out.

Among the advice religions offer, Tibetan Buddhism takes an interesting approach—a guidebook to death. Like a travel guide, it describes in detail what we'll encounter during our dying and the journey to rebirth—or even better, to Nirvana. *The Tibetan Book of the Dead* teaches believers how to prepare for the transition, how to behave in the in-between place, ways to confront fear, and what our destination might be. For believers, this is very reassuring. And for many of us outside the tradition, it's a valuable reminder that we can find ways to confront our mortality with clear and hopeful wisdom.

Planning our routes to the end, and choosing companions to take it with us, is part of a mature spiritual practice. We learn from many faiths that to give our final journey the attention that we would give to any trip adds depth and meaning to our living.

Many who travel keep journals or blogs. Wouldn't it be interesting to write down, draw, or imagine how we'd like this leg of our journey to go—what roads of forgiveness, compassion, and peace we might travel?

# Tend Your Vineyard

It's true, some wines improve with age. But only if
the grapes were good in the first place.

—ABIGAIL VAN BUREN

Some of life's most pleasurable things improve as they grow
older—like cheese, woodwinds, and Scotch. Harvested, rip-
ened, seasoned things are among earth's great delights. Why
not people, too?

To see if you're on your way to becoming an earthly delight,
check your crop and see what you need to become a stellar
vintage. It's never too early to start becoming the best grapes
we can be.

A good grape is cultivated, weeded, pruned, and given what
it needs to grow. It is juicy, rich in sugars, full of the sun's
warmth and the earth's minerals. Good grapes ripen on the
vine—and they come in bunches.

We need to be tended by those who'll help us become our
juiciest selves. We depend on the well-being of the whole vine-
yard, sharing the sun and the shade. We soak up water, nutri-
ents, and the sun's rays; we take healthy swigs from our roots.
We aren't afraid of a little sweetness or acidity. We are true to
ourselves and our unfolding.

And then we give ourselves over to the yeasty process of fermentation. Fermenting is a process of allowing different elements to interact with one another to create something new—beer from barley, say, or sour dough from wheat. Our spirits can perform this level of transformation through the process of reflection, meditation, or rumination. Allowing these forces to work on all the richness of our lives helps us express more fully all the flavorful layers we've acquired for the enjoyment of all.

# Forever True

Every happiness is the child of a separation
it did not think it could survive.

— RAINER MARIA RILKE

We all wish for life to stay the same. And when forces beyond
our control threaten our integrity, we beg for a way to stay true
to ourselves, though to do so often requires radical change.
We may find our deepest needs answered in ways we can't
imagine.

The Greek myth of the nymph Daphne serves as a timeless
witness to this truth. She is forced to change to survive the
relentless pursuit of the god Apollo. A sympathetic goddess
changes her into a laurel tree to save her from violation. Her
virtue assured, Daphne is changed forever. How does anyone
survive such loss, such deep transformation? Rilke's verses
offer a response: Just as Daphne surrendered her human form
to keep her selfhood, we too can be brave enough to surrender one form of happiness for another. It involves yielding to
the powers of change, trusting to our own resilience.

The old myth reminds us of what we forget when we hang
on too tightly to happiness: that there can be no yin of joy
without the yang of loss. While we don't wish pain on anyone,

we hear and read accounts of the deepening appreciation and joy in life that loss can give us. For example, while Daphne lost her physical mobility, she kept her integrity and gained new relationships with wind and water, with the other beings of the woods. When we embrace such possibilities, we know that the children of separation are ours to adopt.

# The Tribe

We have learned much during our long lives. Yet there we were in our old age, thinking that we had done our share in life.

— Velma Wallis

How many of us, influenced by a leisure-worshipping culture, imagine that there will come a day when we have "done our share in life"? We may live for that day, putting in our time, watching the clock. Or we might wake one day feeling that we no longer have much to contribute to today's fast-moving, technically complex world. Either way seems to inspire entropy, the great winding down of vitality into nothingness.

This quotation from Wallis comes from her interpretation of an Athabascan legend. Her story describes how two older women stopped contributing to the collective life of the tribe. The leaders of the nomadic community made the tough decision to leave the women behind one particularly rough winter. The legend tells some harsh truths about survival, age, and the saving instinct to grab hope by the tail and hang on tight.

The women are not close to anyone, not even each other, until sheer need forces them together. Each helps the other find the will to live in spite of rejection by the community. In sharing their skills to find food and stay warm, they discover many inner resources, like bravery and wisdom. In salvaging their lives, they recover their dignity and they treasure their connection to others. They prove themselves stronger than they imagined, in spite of the afflictions of old age. Having discovered their strength, they find it is needed by their people.

We all get caught up in worry at times, especially if we live alone. We might wonder: Where is my share? What do others contribute? What is my role? These are universal questions, but they are not always the most helpful.

We can learn much from those living in the harsher environments. They live their belief that we are all connected—people, animals, insects, plants, and planet. This means hard work, and sometimes hard choices. Like the two brave women, we need to keep hold of and value the wisdom and skills we've accumulated in our lifetimes, keep them honed, and be ready to share them so all may thrive.

Perhaps we can ponder the twenty-first century versions of these ancient questions: What is of the utmost importance to me and to my community? Do the children know how to catch fish in the winter? Whose future depends on our stores of knowledge? What skills and power do I have to offer others?

# Gracious Living

Life is a gift for which we are grateful.

— MARJORIE MONTGOMERY

Who can resist opening a present? Shaking the box, guessing aloud what it might be, snapping the tape, and unknotting the bright ribbon?

If we gave something wonderful to someone we cherished and they passed it on unopened, we'd feel hurt. At best we'd consider them thrifty re-gifters. But when the gift is love, we often pass it on unopened. There's so much risk and so great a chance for surprise that we tend to let it go by — even passing on the love offered to us when we were brought into existence. In refusing to open gifts of love, we refuse the gift of living fully. What an insult to the Giver.

And let's also consider the gift of death. Passing on this gift unopened — well, who *wouldn't* do that? We don't know what's inside, or we think we know and are frightened out of our wits.

It seems unlikely, but death might be a great gift after all. A brave time, a time for tender honesty, for making amends, for saying thanks for the gift of love, for giving our last gifts, and for saying good-bye. Our relationship with the Spirit deepens through living with grace and gratitude—just as it is with all our relationships.

# Unmoored

So throw off the bowlincs. Sail away from the safe
harbor. Catch the trade winds in your sails.
Explore. Dream. Discover.

—Anonymous

Picture the end of a journey at sea. Sails furled and bowlines
neatly tied at the dock. Ruddy sun setting. As we grow older,
is the primary goal to find a safe place to anchor and hunker
down, to become an armchair sailor or a landlubber? Is this
what we've crossed oceans for?

Clamber back into the boat. Twain, navigating great losses
along with adventure and delight, knew the romance of great
rivers and oceans, new ports, and people. He also knew that
to sail means to acknowledge the limits of our control—we
steer with rudder, lines, and sail, yet must defer to wind and
wave.

As adults, we dream, explore, and discover; we benefit from
all kinds of knowing that we may not have had as teenagers
or young adults. We have experience with tides. We're more
humble about what we can't control, like weather; we bring
greater insight to our discoveries because we have more experiences and relationships to draw on. We may even have greater

physical awareness, or at least appreciation of our strengths and our limits. And we may also be wilder dreamers, caring less about what others think.

To be moored in comfort may be our dream of old age when we're young and struggling to capture the winds of self-discovery. But living safely at anchor is hardly a life. Living requires riding a full sail, honing our craft, using the wind, and trusting the currents to bring us to new awareness.

# Crossing the River

Jacob was left alone; and a man wrestled with him
until daybreak. When the man saw that he did not
prevail against Jacob, he struck him on the hip
socket; and Jacob's hip was put out of joint as he
wrestled with him.

—GENESIS 32:24–25

We can all identify with Jacob, nowhere more in his story
than in this passage, where he is alone. He's fearful of the
next day's encounter with his brother—a man he wronged
long ago. A mixture of doubt, guilt, regret, and fear keep him
from sleep during that long night by the river—flowing
between his past and his future. He struggles hard with the
known and the unknown, as many of us do.

But after a long hard night, he is blessed with a new name,
Israel, fulfilling a divine promise made to his forefathers. Limp-
ing, he bears this new identity forward, for his descendants.
What a blessing, to persevere long enough, with faith enough,
to keep our covenant with the future!

Jacob's limp marks his struggle and, for the rest of his life,
signifies how he prevailed in his faith. As we get older, we
accumulate physical signs of all we have endured, of our own

wrestling with our humanity, with our failures to keep our highest promises, and with our hopes to be and do better. These signs may not be visible to others, but we bear them nonetheless.

When we limp forward, hoping to right old wrongs, to ask forgiveness, to seek reconciliation, our efforts will be blessed. In so doing, we are renamed, reborn, however broken we may feel. We may not know with whom we have wrestled, but we will carry the sacred knowledge of our struggle and of our prevailing—and our descendants will not forget.

# Giving Up the Stick

Jim was so nervous about having a beginner at
the controls that he'd never yielded either stick or
rudder to my command. . . . The plane had dual
controls. . . . Occasionally Jim had even congratu-
lated me on the skill with which he had executed
a landing.

— RUSSELL BAKER

If you have ever taught a young person to drive, you remember the gut-tightening anxiety you had to suppress while you
gave instructions. Passing on a skill that involves a large and
complex machine or system can be challenging, as shown in
this memory of a young Air Force cadet. Baker was eager to
learn to fly, but his flight instructor, Jim, refused to hand over
the controls, despite the safety feature of back-up controls.

Because of Jim's lack of trust in his student and in his own
teaching skills, Baker had little confidence. He tensed up,
and failed his first flight exam. This episode highlights how
teaching requires several levels of trust. Spiritual preparation
for becoming a mentor, while often overlooked, can enhance
the experience for everyone.

The inner work needed for successful teaching is offered by many spiritual traditions. It involves learning that we don't have to be in control to attain what we most desire. Artist Walter Anderson says, "We're never so vulnerable than when we trust someone—but paradoxically, if we cannot trust, neither can we find love or joy."

A vital skill in passing on our knowledge, just as in acquiring knowledge, is letting go of the ego's attachment to outcomes. Trust in ourselves, in others, and in life itself, is key to sharing our wisdom with the future.

# Stop the World?

Whether we are talking about a bird's song, a breath, or a person's life, the truth is clear, before us every moment: this is a world in which nothing lasts.

—JOYCE KORNBLATT

We don't like to hear that life is change. Today's technology appeals to our deepest desire—to capture each crimson leaf as it falls to earth, every trill of every wood thrush, and every grin ever grinned—enabling us to record and store it all forever.

But do we really want our lives stored in the cloud of forever? Often, absorbed in boxing up our moments, we miss them because we are too busy behind the camera or fiddling with the recording mechanism on our phone. Scrapbooks can be wonderful tools for recalling moments and images, but they are as advertised: books of scraps, however artfully presented.

We create whole, meaningful, beautiful lives one grain at a time, just as Tibetan monks create sacred paintings in the colorful sands of their mandalas. To begin the process, priests invoke the powers of goodness and consecrate the space; they bless the creative process and bring to it their prayerful attention.

21

While creating the mandalas, the monks pray, chant, meditate, and play music. They take painstaking days to bring these jewel-like windows into the web of existence. Using delicate tools, they move the colored sands, a few grains at a time, creating order out of chaos, beauty out of earth. Soon after they finish, after more chanting and prayers, the monks sweep the glorious colors, shapes, and vital lines away with thick brushes. All that remains is a faint outline and some muddied bits of sand. This sand is then gathered and returned to a river, which then flows out to the oceans of the world, blessing us with, and reminding us of, the oneness of creation.

This is one tradition's idea of what life is all about—impermanence. The importance of creating mandalas is not to show off great skill and patience. The spiritually enriching act lies in being willing to sweep the beauty away, trusting that our unbreakable connection to the cosmos abides forever.

# Bring Your Waders

His heart is an educated swamp,
and he is mindful of his garden.

— STANLEY KUNITZ

The heart—seat of love, desire, bliss, and disappointments—
really is a swamp. Swamps are fertile places that act as puri-
fiers of water, nurseries for the new, and buffers of transitions.
Our hearts are *educated* swamps because, like our minds, they
hold encyclopedias of experience and thesauruses of memories. They are nearly as full of nerve endings as our brains,
and they can be just as wise.

Swamps are also places where life is digested back into
minerals and mud. Decay is a kind of fallowness, the process
of life returning to the womb. To know about decay and fertility, planting and pruning, is to know about ourselves, our
created being and our fate. As Kunitz knows from decades of
practice, to know a garden is to know ourselves more completely. Such knowledge includes both the facts and the mystery of living and dying. In accepting this knowledge, we find
peace.

It's a stereotype—the elderly tending gardens—and yet it's
a powerful image. We can use our discretionary time for

activities that heal us and the world around us. We become mindful of what grows, where living things thrive, and the kinds of nurture—or benign neglect—they need to become what they were meant to be. How lucky any of us would be to have "mindful gardeners" watching over us!

Helping to create life within the cycle of the natural world—and not fighting it—is one of the secrets of growing older while staying young in spirit. Aging gracefully means mucking about, awake to the garden we tend.

# Sweeter Than Wine

The wide, the bleak abyss
Shifted with our slow kiss.

—THEODORE ROETHKE

Few things feel more luxurious than a slow kiss. Sharing physical delight means actively listening to our bodies. Caressing and holding someone, being caressed and held, help us know we are desired, loved, wholly wanted.

Stereotypes of aging don't usually include physical passion, or if they do, hold it up to ridicule. Our physical bodies change, of course, and sometimes our desires change as well. When we entered puberty we had no idea what desires and needs would arise in us, or how our physical selves might be held and satisfied. Many of us sublimated our desires in confusion, or we fumbled, misfired, or got stuck at various points on our sexual learning curves. But those who cared about us supported us through these experiments.

Later in life, we can become more accepting of our changing needs and desires. Of course, slow kisses are vital to our sense of well-being—perhaps even more so as we age, because we know to delight in love when we have it.

Our bodies, including our senses, often lead us to the eternal. Many other things we do lift us beyond time's touch as well. When we express ourselves through creating works of art, athletics, or deep conversations, our physical immersion in existence fully releases our passion for life, and our attunement with its vitality and rhythms.

As we grow older, we cherish the opportunities for such engagement but we also appreciate shared physical expression. We understand how physical tenderness, passion, and love can transform a bleak horizon into a gentle landscape. When we spend time enjoying one another's physical beings, we embody the holy embrace of the universe.

# We Would Be One

I recalled that in every great spiritual tradition
there is an emphasis on remembering. Christians
speak of the recollected heart and of being in a
state of recollection. *Smirti* in Sanskrit, *sati* in
Pali, *drenpa* in Tibetan—all mean to remember—
literally to "re-member" or to "re-collect" ourselves,
to stop all our striving outward, to pull ourselves
together, to be connected inside—body, heart,
and mind.

— TRACY COCHRAN

When we think about remembering, we might conjure up
something like a front porch, family, and iced tea served
sweet with stories. Many of us think of remembering as slow-
ing us down, or a luxury. Others can't curb our skepticism
about how great the past was; for some of us sadness, regret,
or hurt keep the past locked up tight.

We might not be able, therefore, to re-member ourselves,
re-collect our whole selves, without the assurance of a compassionate space in which to do this soul work. If we seek
support, if we make the time, if we move always toward
loving-kindness for ourselves and others, we may find a way

to bring the lonely or broken parts of ourselves—heart, mind, and spirit—together. Yet we can't grow more whole if there are parts of ourselves thrown or locked away.

The goddess Isis, after many tears and prayers, searched the world for the dismembered body of her murdered husband Osiris. Miraculously, from her recollected love, a divine new being was born, their child Horus. When will you make time to gather your whole being and bring something new into the world? When were you planning to get off the treadmill and gather yourself, composing the most complete self you are capable of being?

Some say that illness or approaching death catalyzes this level of reflection, but we don't need to wait for that trauma to achieve greater wholeness. Why avoid being re-called to your self? Why not listen now, so you can dance the cosmic dance and teach the steps to others while you can still kick and twirl, shimmy and bow?

# Unwinding

I teach my eyes to hear, my ears to see
How body from spirit slowly does unwind.

— THEODORE ROETHKE

At the beginning of our growing, adults teach us to see with our eyes and hear with our ears; we take in bottle and blanket, woof and meow, bike and fire engine. As we enter adulthood, our ability to actively hear and see the world around us grows dull—we're often too busy to notice it.

We can adopt a spiritual practice of waking up our senses. This isn't a response to blurring vision or diminished hearing. It's about the need, especially as we grow older, to re-awaken the part of ourselves that learns about the world through sight and sound and smell and sensation.

How often do you really listen to the squirrel chattering on the sidewalk or notice the quality of the light streaming through a window? One way to recapture that fascination with the world that we had as children is to be creative and notice what's happening around us in new and different ways. Questions like "What does the sky sound like?" and "What is the shape of a purr?" wake up parts of ourselves that have been dormant these many years.

29

In the Genesis creation story, God breathes across the waters of chaos that cover the earth, and the first thing his breath creates is light, which allows us to see. Living sensually keeps us from taking the landscape of our lives for granted.

# Let's Shake on It

> If you look deeply into the palm of your hand, you will see your parents and all generations of your ancestors. All of them are alive in this moment. Each is present in your body. You are the continuation of each of these people.
>
> —Thich Nhat Hanh

When we look at our hands, it's usually because we're grooming our nails or taking care of minor injuries. We might occasionally notice changes in our skin and nails—creases, thickening joints, or liver spots. Sadly, we tend to try to hide them or rub them out with rejuvenating ointments.

Try this: Cradle one hand in the other, palm up. Take a few minutes to contemplate your palm. Palmistry is the art of predicting the future through studying the lines formed there, but we can go deeper.

Observe your palm. Observe this web of your living and doing, and imagine the palms of parents, grandparents, and all the greats, back to the palms of the original mother and father of us all. What a precious and ancient fabric our skin is, born of millions and millions of separate selves in communities that blossomed over centuries of seasons.

And from our open palms, from all that we offer the world of our good work, our creativity and loving-kindness, the blossoming will continue forward in time and through time, generation to generation.

In classical Eastern-style meditation, the hands rest palm upward on the lower thighs. This ancient gesture speaks of both engagement and surrender. An open palm is not usually a default position—we must make the effort, holding out our openness, like offering a hand to a stranger. For this symbolic opening of our hearts, too, we have our ancestors to thank.

At our fingertips, we carry our most important connections, and a key to our place in the web of life.

# Either/Or Wave

> Whereas human intuition, and its embodiment in classical physics, envisions a reality in which things are always definitely one way or another, quantum mechanics describes a reality in which things sometimes hover in a haze of being partly one way and partly another.
>
> —BRIAN GREENE

We may or may not understand classic physics, but we do understand the notion "this way *or* that." We've all heard the expression "My way or the highway." But now cutting-edge science tells us that everything can operate in a vague and wishy-washy manner.

Most of us function best when things are definite. We enjoy our ability to grasp the rules that help us function in the world, rules governing everything from bowling balls to electricity to growing soybeans. We like the orderliness of electrons orbiting protons and neutrons, like they did in the diagrams in our old textbooks.

But it turns out that that's not the way the universe actually works. The real universe contains mysteries we can only hope to penetrate. Its basic elements are both particle and wave, matter and energy. Sometimes the nature of those elements depends on whether someone's looking, where in its trajectory the particle/wave may be, or if a wave/particle light years away has swerved or flipped from one state to the other.

It's a mystery, our mystery—for our lives are also not clearly defined, static elements. The course of our lives may depend on who's looking at what, the unleashed forces of a solar flare, or even a distant sneeze.

We can't see the bones of our everyday universe, and the older we grow, the more we understand that there are forces at work that we'll never completely know. As we grow into that wisdom, we may find it easier to bow to the Mystery and live into its sacred Both/And.

# Travelers

Journeying God,
pitch your tent with mine

— KATE COMPSTON

Some of us may not believe in God or gods, or even see the need for such a belief. Others of us harbor cautious doubt. Still others find ourselves praying in times of need without understanding to what or whom we pray.

All belief is rooted in choice; if we choose to address a divinity, we may gain a sense of peace. Compston's words are one kind of prayer. Like many prayers, it joins us in community. It also addresses our universal desire for strength and connection. The final line of the prayer goes, "Help me to find myself as I walk in others' shoes," reinforcing the hope that the holy resides in the journey into relationship.

Maybe the idea of a god arose from the smoke of a traveler's campfire. The speaker here knows the journey will not be easy—it may be marked by homesickness, alienation, dangers, or uncertainty—and so she invokes a steadfast and loving fellow traveler.

We can be plagued by doubt and lack of courage even when we have companions. These feelings can force us to turn back, to retreat to old habits and to a narrower existence unless we call on other resources. So why not a traveling god? Why not a divine force that walks with us, slogging along beside us, hauling a backpack and tent uphill and across creeks? How about a god who shares moleskins and coffee, listens to our stories around the fire at night, and maybe even snores a bit?

We are all on a journey, and our path is not always clear. We can't be sure where or how our journey will end. We will meet all kinds of fellow creatures—good, bad, and indifferent, human and animal—along our way. The company of a traveling god offers constancy, comfort, and joy as we journey into deeper understanding of ourselves.

# No Supermen Need Apply

As I wrestled with cancer and its treatment I
wanted to be more to my sons than just Dad the
patient, their father unexpectedly undone by disease. I wanted to try to be a role model, wanted
them to know that it was necessary to talk about it,
laugh about it and, yes, sometimes cry about it.

— DANA JENNINGS

The most invisible part of coping with disease or disability
may be the struggle with identity. Others may see the physical
manifestations but not know about the endless questions we ask
ourselves: Who am I now? How can I help others to see there's
so much more to me than my wheelchair or lack of sight?

For all the young people in our lives, we are models for
how to be human, whether we know it or not. That's hum-an,
as in *humus*, down-to-earth, out of clay and back again,
humane and humble. As adults, it's humbling to know we're
being closely watched — and we are, because young people
are so eager to know how to grow up, how to rise up out of
the clay of our beginnings into the air and light.

And back to earth we go again, sometimes before we are
ready. Having a terminal disease helps Jennings know just

how much he has to give his children. In illness, we are more than just a patient, a container for medication, a subject of diagnoses. Our bonds with others do not dry up and disappear when someone sticks an intravenous needle in our arm, or because we can't bike fifteen miles at a stretch like we used to.

In her exploration of the roots of compassion, author Karen Armstrong has discovered a truth that goes as far back as Confucianism: If we deny our own pain, it enables us to deny the pain and suffering of others. And it is in this sense, she goes on to say, that compassion saves us. Jennings does not fail to see the opportunity in his experience to save himself. He also helps his children to learn compassion through his powerful example.

We're flesh and blood, so different from those fantastic plastic action figures with super powers that children enjoy. And with our children watching us, we hug, talk, laugh, and shed tears in the face of death. We show them by our actions all the ways that human beings can be strong and yet vulnerable, brave and yet afraid, sure and also uncertain. Being our most human selves provides salvation for our children.

Jennings has passed through fire in his efforts to stay alive—not merely to survive but to be present to himself, his family, and to his community of fellow human beings. Like him, we are more than patients—we are teachers as well as students of our humanity.

# Simplify

However mean your life, meet it and live it; do not
shun it and call it hard names. It is not so bad. . . .
It looks poorest when you are richest.

— Henry David Thoreau

Many of us have fantasized escaping the tangles of our lives
and finding a simpler way of being—close to nature, perhaps,
or at least more in tune with her rhythms. Thoreau commands
respect to this day for taking this fantasy and making it real.

If you last read *Walden* in high school, this might be the
right time to return to that journal of life at the edge of a
pond in nineteenth-century Concord. If you've never read it,
go directly to the library and enjoy a great read. The experience can reawaken what we know to be true but may be afraid
to act on: that to live fully and meaningfully we don't need to
toil away at jobs we hate, we don't need to have fancy homes,
and we don't have to spend time with people with whom we
have nothing in common.

If we want true fulfillment, we need to connect with
nature—an experience that causes us to be more intimate
with time, and yet also beyond its reach. We need to connect
with our fellow human beings, too, but not as often, or as

many, as we might think. Thoreau did not become a hermit, but he did enjoy a greater balance of social and reflective time.

If we do not have a lot of money—if we do not own our own home, or a car—it is hard in a consumer-driven culture not to feel poor and hard done by. But Thoreau is right to urge us to avoid bitterness. In recent published interviews, some of the richest people in our nation consistently report feeling isolated, unhappy, and dissatisfied with their lives in some way.

The Transcendentalists provide us with a wonderful antidote to the poison of unbridled materialism. Contemplating the wealth supplied by the natural world offers a peace no money can buy.

# Finding Ourselves in Low Places

The supreme good is like water,
which nourishes all things without trying to.

— TAO TE CHING

We often think it's important to carve our paths, like a river barreling to the ocean. When we connect with others, we are usually focused on performing some action—scheduling a meeting, giving an invitation, getting or giving information. The *Tao Te Ching* reminds us that our essential purpose is to become nourishment for all things. Our purpose in life isn't to race to a goal, to be first, or to be the richest. We serve our first and best purpose by remembering to be like water.

Water naturally finds itself in low places. Its essence is to flow, to go graciously where it is needed, and to be present for all that need it. A low place, like a vernal pool or bog, is usually overlooked, considered unworthy, as we roar and babble along, hurried by the flotsam and jetsam of our days. But water that comes to rest, that serves its essence, gives birth to such exquisite and rare beings as spotted salamanders and spring peepers.

Why do we hurry? How can we provide nourishment to those we race past? The more we learn about this cosmic web of life, the more we realize that every part is significant.

Lakes, puddles, oceans, and birdbaths—all kinds of water—are of the essence of life. Even our brains are 85 percent water. This marvelous mixture of hydrogen and oxygen chemically enables us to think, feel, and do.

Pondering water might serve as a walking meditation. Moving deliberately, following the contours of the earth in our neighborhood, we can repeat, "I am from and of water, and I, too, can imitate that supreme good."

# *If Two Are Good*

Two are better than one, because they have a good
reward for their toil. For if they fall, one will lift up
the other; but woe to one who is alone and falls
and does not have another to help. Again, if two lie
together, they keep warm; but how can one keep
warm alone? And though one might prevail against
another, two will withstand one. A threefold cord is
not quickly broken.

—Ecclesiastes 4:9–12

An orphan, a stranger in a crowded town, a newly widowed
person. Our most animal selves share in their cries, "How
can one keep warm alone?" and "Woe to one who is alone."
Think of mice, their soft furry bodies curled into a living nest.
Imagine pet store ferrets or puppies sleeping against each
other like spoons. While some of us thrive primarily on time
and space to be alone, most of us do best when our solitude
is balanced with time in the company of others.

As we retire, experience the empty nest, move, or otherwise leave the familiar, we become more intentional about
keeping our spirits warm, our souls productive, and our hearts
bound to other hearts.

Imagine making of your life a three-fold or eight-fold cord. You must choose your material from the most resilient vines, the silkiest grasses, and the strongest fibers. You will need lots of space in order to shape the cords individually, and then you will need to braid them together. The separate cords become one cord, but each remains distinctive. Once finished, the braided cord must be treated with care, used judiciously and, always, gratefully.

Think of being snugly woven into a thickly braided rope. Intertwining relationships keep us from unraveling, and help us to do compassionate deeds we couldn't do alone. They also help keep us accountable to something or someone beyond ourselves.

This kind of interdependence makes us stronger as individuals and more responsive to one another in community.

# The Myth of the Bad Day

I promised myself that I wouldn't have a bad day
for the rest of my life. If someone was wasting my
time, I'd excuse myself and walk away. If a situation
bothered me or refused to get resolved, I'd shrug
and move on.

— PETER BARTON

Having a bad day? It's a common excuse for grumpy and
even rude behavior, for giving up on others and ourselves.
How amazing it would be to never have one again! How life
changing to make that vow. Well, this is the vow a person
dying from cancer made to himself and his family. Barton,
a father of three, worked hard at overcoming the disease but
received a dire prognosis on the cusp of his fiftieth birthday.

When he learned that his cancer had returned with a ven-
geance, he became depressed and self-pitying. He complained
that life meant nothing. And then his wife challenged him to
continue living as he, a vibrant, athletic entrepreneur, always
had—full-throttle. She inspired him to find or make meaning of the life he was given.

A self-proclaimed doer, not a thinker or spiritual guy, he
wrote that his cancer made him reflective, enriching his life

in ways he never imagined possible. He gained many insights, including an understanding that, while we can't always control events, we can choose what we make of them. So this became his practice, to make every day a good day by choosing how to use his time, who to spend it with, and how to react to what he couldn't control.

We don't need to have a terminal disease to know that our days are given to us, not earned. We all can vow to embrace life's twists and turns as opportunities for choosing happiness.

# Idle Worship

Too many people who lose others—mothers,
fathers, children, friends—become people who use
grief as a tent pole for their life. They cherish it
almost, they clutch it to them, they never let it go.

—ART LINKLETTER

Imagine a sturdy oak pole, tall enough to lift the heavy canvas
of your life. It looks like a shelter, sure, but it's not as strong
as it looks. One fierce wind or downpour, and you are swept
away.

Clutching onto our emotions, no matter how powerful they
may be, can lead us to erect a spiritual home that is no stronger than that tent. Grief—due to death, loss, or heartbreak—
is one of those emotions universal enough to easily arouse
sympathy in others. If we're not careful, our sorrow can become
our tent pole, our whole identity, without providing any real
strength.

The image of tent poles also evokes long-ago tent revivals
in which masses of people were roused to religious enthusi-
asm through appeals to their emotions. Perhaps this kind of
worship is sustaining, but it may leave us craving more and

more instead of moving us toward a deeper connection to our innermost selves or to the divine.

Anger, grief, and other strong emotions are important, to be sure. Imagine not feeling them, and how isolated we'd be from others as well as ourselves. Our emotions keep us attuned to others and to our deepest values; they remind us of who we are and how much others mean to us. In one sense, we live in a sea of emotions that ebb and flow around and through us, nourishing us and sweeping away toxins.

But strong feelings and the rush that comes with them can become addictive. You may find it helpful, during a contemplative moment, to reflect on what you might be clinging to. Have you made sadness the center pole of your life? What are you holding onto so tightly that it crowds out a fuller range of feelings and experiences?

When choosing what to cherish, be sure that it is worthy of your devotion.

# Troubled Waters

Wade in the water,
Wade in the water, children,
Wade in the water,
God's gonna trouble the water.

—AFRICAN-AMERICAN SPIRITUAL

At first blush, these lyrics seem contradictory: Why wade in the water if that's where God's going to bring turbulence? But these words speak to seeking physical and spiritual freedom, whatever the cost. They are about trust in the divine power that guides us in our quest for it. When chased by hounds, slaves knew that wading in the water provided cover by erasing human scent.

American slaves had little but their faith, and they saw their struggles reflected in the story of Moses and the Israelites. The escaping Hebrew slaves hesitated beside the sea, weighing whom to trust before wading in. Moses? Pharaoh's forgiveness? Yahweh? They came to believe that if they followed the person who followed God, the waters covering the path would be pushed aside, making way for them to go on to a new land.

Whether or not we believe in one god, or many, or none, this song comes from deep within the human heart, urging us to trust in something greater, to believe that somehow we will be led to a place where we can live with dignity and respect. And if we feel we've reached that glorious shore, this song calls us to remember those who live in bondage—political, mental, or economic—and to help trouble the waters by reaching out to them on their journey to a better life.

# It Doesn't Take Much

But a handful of pine-seed will cover mountains
with the green majesty of forest. And so I too will
set my face to the wind and throw my handful of
seed on high.

— FIONA MACLEOD

How do whole forests get planted? How does one seed give
birth to the awesome biosphere of a giant redwood? What if
we don't have a handful of seed, but only one? What good
does it do to plant one tree when a whole mountainside lies
bare?

The question of reforesting bare land may call to mind the
story of Wangari Maathai, a Kenyan woman who won the
Nobel Peace prize a few years ago for leading a movement to
plant thousands of seeds. She noticed that her beloved land
was being deforested and that no one was planting trees. She
began by planting a flame tree outside her home. She started
with one seed.

But as she planted more and encouraged others to do so,
more than trees were sown: understanding about the earth
and stewardship was also planted. Asking why trees were being
destroyed and who was destroying them started a political

movement. Maathai said, "It's the little things citizens do. That's what will make the difference. My little thing is planting trees."

Of course, it wasn't easy. She had to stand firm against the political and economic forces that threaten many new ideas. She used the opposition of those in power to spread her ideas. She used what she had and what she was given to make one change that could help save the world she loves for her children and her children's children.

Throwing a handful of seed seems like a simplistic gesture. But the effects of one gesture ripple outward. The seeds sprout, provide food for animals, whose droppings provide food for insects and fertilizer for other plants. Those that survive grow into small trees, providing shade for the friable earth, roots to anchor the soil and catch the rain, and branches to break the wind. More leaves mean more oxygen, and the whole means a richer habitat for wildlife. For Maathai, the most important effect is the restoration of the good green world she so values.

Imagine one thing you'd like to leave to the children. Imagine planting that one seed of love, of beauty, of freedom.

# All Lives Flow On

No single thing abides; but all things flow.
Fragment to fragment clings—the things thus grow.

— LUCRETIUS

From the perspective of our daily lives, it seems that some things stay put, like mountains and oceans. Science, however, demonstrates that this is not true. We've found the fossils of tropical plants far from jungles and the imprints of seashells thousands of miles from any sea. The earth and ice hold records of the multitudes of species that lived their eons and then disappeared.

"No single thing abides," least of all us. But the poet and Epicurean philosopher Lucretius did not write his book to cause despair. His philosophy resembles Buddhist thought; he wants us to recognize the transience of things so we will not suffer so much in life, so we won't be enslaved by worshipping what is, and so we won't be so afraid of death that we cannot enjoy life.

But Lucretius's gleanings from Epicurus seem counter to joy: don't eat fancy food, eat very moderately, and abstain from sex. Indulging in these pleasures brings suffering to the body, heart, and spirit. A well-lived, contented life for Epicurus was monk-like. He understood that even knowledge is fluid and transient, so for him the life of ideas was a kind of play.

However we decide to live, the health of our spirit depends on how tightly we cling to things and names—and how willing we are to let them go.

# Gather the Spirit

It was not easy, but eventually we gathered
enough courage to assess our talents, experience,
and potential influence in affecting some of the
social and political issues in which we were still
interested.

— JIMMY CARTER

Self-assessment is never easy, and it would be understand-
able if folks who've been active in a variety of ways all their
lives, like Jimmy and Roslyn Carter, chose in their later years
to withdraw. Leading a quiet life, devoted to pursuing hobbies,
should be fulfilling after a lifetime of pursuing a demanding
career, raising children, or being involved in the community.
But many who retire and withdraw find inactivity harmful
to the spirit; we've all heard stories of people who languish
when their formal work lives end.

Throughout our lives, looking closely and honestly at our
choices takes courage. In *The Wizard of Oz*, the Cowardly
Lion cries out for the quality he knows he lacks—the one attri-
bute that would help him in his role as king of the forest. But
in the end, his honesty, loyalty, and compassion are revealed
as the *true* measures of his courage.

Sometimes we find our courage in the moment. Faced with a crisis, we don't think; we act bravely and selflessly. These actions are often rewarded by public accolades and labels like "hero." But there's another kind of courage that we may access once we're less encumbered by the demands of our younger days—spiritual courage.

Courageous spirits practice compassion by taking honest looks at themselves, their skills and their experience, as well as their ability to communicate and persuade. We must forgive our weaknesses and limits, and be true to ourselves. We must be honest about what we truly care about, or our commitment will wobble and falter.

It takes spiritual strength to approach life again and again with passion and commitment. It takes courage to rise above indifference and to love deeply and widely this untamable, awe-inspiring thing called life.

# Opening into Silence

Silence also heals. It heals by and through itself
so that to enter it is to enter a process of self-
healing. We notice this when we move beyond
ego-consciousness to discover that silence fills
the inner form of our body, which becomes a
body of silence, transparent and open to the
greater body of silence that is the universe itself.

—Christopher Bamford

Bamford, in his review of a book about silence, introduces us
to a paradox not so much about silence but about what it
means to be healed. It helps to know that the word *heal*
means "to be whole," a root thousands of years deep in human
understanding.

It's not news, of course, that to feel whole, complete, we
have to move beyond our sense of self. But since ancient
times, intentionally entering silence has been the vehicle for
letting go of the ego. When we embody silence, that absence/
presence that reflects the universal mystery, we first tune out
the chatter of our wants and desires, and we gain a sense of
unity with all that is.

Embodying silence isn't easy. We seem to enjoy being busy, and most of us don't sit still much. But if we seek to be transformed, doing the same busy things over and over generally doesn't work out well. Which is why silence—entering it, maintaining it, and becoming it—lies at the heart of many of the world's religious traditions. Just as noise has the power to affect our lives—think loudspeakers, judges' hammers, or train whistles—so does silence.

Some of us need, and know we need, a certain amount of silence every day. As we age, we often find ourselves requiring more space and more silence in which to grow into all the experiences and understandings we have gained.

We may at times escape our own thoughts and worries by avoiding silence. Yet to become fully present to the Mystery, we must open ourselves to the greater silence from which we come and to which we return.

# Wizard School

There is only one thing for it then—to learn. Learn
why the world wags and what wags it. That is the
only thing which the poor mind can never exhaust,
never alienate, never be tortured by, never fear or
distrust, and never dream of regretting. Learning is
the thing for you. Look at what a lot of things there
are to learn.

—T.H. WHITE

You may recall how the future King Arthur was taught by
the wizard Merlin. Like most of us, the legendary wizard is
excited to offer his wisdom to a promising young person. Sharing hard-won knowledge with someone delights us. We hope
that we'll save at least one soul from reinventing the wheel.
We have created some shape out of the chaos of our lives and
can now hold that form up for others.

The list of things to learn is long and Merlin's tone is
urgent. He realizes that time is short. Cursed with living his
life backwards, he knows that he'll be seduced, exploited, and
imprisoned by the enchantress Vivian, unable to help himself, his king, or the kingdom. Teaching young Arthur prevents despair.

Now that we are old enough to have known betrayal, loss, and urgency, what do we do? Where do we start to pass along our help to others? Merlin's long list of things for Arthur to learn ends with the mundane—learn to plough—but begins with the purpose of all learning, to figure out "why the world wags and what wags it."

Merlin goes on to show Arthur how, when we learn about things that matter, we delve deeply into the ordinary tasks of living—even something as basic as plowing. And he teaches him that what appears to be ordinary is complicated and interconnected with other kinds of knowledge. For instance, when and how to prepare the soil to grow vegetables leads us to know about dirt and air and sun, about our interfusing with the smallest and greatest things in the solar system, and the wondrous generative power of the earth.

From his long experience, Merlin knows that knowledge is a kind of power. Our curiosity and delving deep keep the world wagging, and lead the next generation to wag the world.

# Stuff

Give thought to giving. Give small things, carefully,
and observe the mental processes going along with
the act of releasing the little thing you liked.

— ROBERT A.F. THURMAN

As we grow older we may find ourselves in possession of a lot
of stuff, especially if we have children or other family members
and if we're blessed with a roomy home. Some of our
stuff has great sentimental value — letters and photos, Grandma's
vase, Dad's old spade — and some of it could be used by
somebody else, like old toys and *National Geographics*. There
are always great reasons for hanging on to things, especially if
they carry fulfilling associations.

On the other hand, stuff can be a ball and chain, requiring
us to do work we might not enjoy just so we can afford to
store, insure, and clean it. Maintaining it might tie up our
free time, even if we don't use it all that often. Psychologically,
its looming presence in our attic or basement can drain
us of energy we might otherwise devote to people, jobs, studies,
hobbies, or volunteering.

Thurman, a Buddhist monk, offers us an interesting and
even harder challenge than decluttering. He invites us to

give away generously—and thoughtfully—the things we love. The practice, done effectively, involves our intention, our asking, "What do I give with this thing I enjoy owning?" To be able to afford to be generous, and to know that it costs us very little, can liberate our spirits. We travel lighter, freer in the heart, when we've experienced the freedom of giving. And we take a first step down the road to becoming ancestors.

# Lessons from Love

Your style is a function of your limitations, more so
than a function of your skills.

—ROSANNE CASH

In an interview about what qualities make music emotive,
the daughter of a famously talented singer shares what she
learned from her father, the secret of his signature communi-
cation style. Johnny Cash, a hard-working, hard-playing, hard-
worshipping man, brought empathy, humor, creativity, and
desire to his music. His life, never easy, grew more complex
as he wrestled with alcohol and other demons.

Cash brought his whole complicated heart to his vocation,
and so when his daughter refers to *style*, I think she means
the unique way in which we each express what matters most
to us. And isn't it a relief to know—after perhaps decades of
trying to erase or temper them—that it may be our weakest
parts, more than our talents, that most help us communicate
with others?

Many people, as they reflect back on their lives, say that what
matters most in a full and meaning-filled life is connection—
to other people, to the natural world, and to the Mystery. We
connect by expressing our appreciation, empathy, thoughts,

63

sympathy, love, and much more. But Rosanne Cash suggests that we connect most effectively and powerfully not through our triumphs, not through brilliant debating technique or perfect melodies, but by sharing the stumblings, doubts, and inadequacies of our hearts.

If we are fortunate, we can become teachers and examples to others in showing them that they are worthy of love by sharing the imperfect wholeness of ourselves.

# What Songs We Sing

[Benjamin Goddard was] a most worthy, upright,
kindly-affectioned man; one who wished well to his
kind, and contributed what in him lay to further
the general good. Such is the verdict of all who
knew him.

— FREDERICK HENRY HEDGE

Benjamin Goddard must have been an amazing person. A
town pillar, he lived to a ripe old age—and Hedge's tribute
wasn't even his eulogy, which had been delivered a week ear-
lier. No, these words were part of a sermon titled "The Les-
sons of Old Age," and Goddard was the chosen model.

If we want to consider how to live the fullest life possible,
this sermon encourages us to look at what we would choose
to leave behind. For some this might be money or land, maybe
an impressive professional portfolio or works of art. These are
wonderful and useful things, but Goddard is remembered for
none of them. His enduring gift was a reliably sustaining and
comforting presence. How many of us will we be remembered
for that when we're gone?

Hedge recalls, "A uniform cheerfulness characterized his
social converse, and a humor which age and infirmity could

not quench." Goddard gave others the benefit of the doubt, always, and "with this were coupled friendly interest in all his acquaintance, lively sympathy with all suffering, hearty good-will toward all mankind." In yet another passage, the minister hails Goddard's integrity; his character was translucent—honest, clear, and pure. Wouldn't you want to bump into him at the post office, or go for coffee with him?

If someone were to write about your life, how would they describe your contributions? What would be the words to the song of your life? What sort of music would help tell your story? What do you want the next verses to hold? Each of us is writing our song now, and some day others may sing it. We are the ones making melodies to be remembered.

# Who Knows You

Give back your heart
to itself, to the stranger who has loved you.

— Derek Walcott

When we've experienced heartbreak or been disillusioned, we can sink into dwelling on our past failures, not even able to think how to mend. We can grow strange, even to ourselves.

Healing these wounds involves falling back in love with ourselves. Often confused with narcissism, self-love has gotten a bad rap. When we finally give our hearts to ourselves we commit to care for and be hospitable to ourselves, no matter what. This means forgiving ourselves for our mistakes and getting back up when we stumble. Just as importantly, we gain compassion for others and their imperfections.

The bigger our hearts the better, metaphorically speaking. When they're open for business, the four chambers of our big, beating hearts have room for all kinds of relationships — with family, friends, and lovers, and also with the source of our lives, however we envision that wonder and power.

Giving our hearts to those who know us by heart means being honest about who we are and loving ourselves still. Healthy hearts are made of tough muscle. They mend when they are given some kind attention, nurtured with the same compassion we hand out to others.

# We're Rich!

Water creates abundance. . . . Abundance comes
not just from how much water flows into a place,
but how well it is used, whether it is available
where and when it is needed, and how many times
it can be recycled and reused before it flows away.

— STARHAWK

We all know that water is a source of life, but we don't often
give it much thought in Western culture unless, as sometimes
happens, a water main breaks and we're without running
water. We notice then!

Starhawk and her friends noticed that the spring that fed
their homes and crops seemed to be drying up. They went
to the source and found that roots were clogging the pipes.
Once cleared, the clean water flowed freely enough to meet
their needs, with a little left over. The spring defines abundance for Starhawk's community—enough for each person's
needs and some left to share.

Perhaps we could adopt this definition of abundance for
ourselves. We might start by defining our needs as those things
that are essential for living decent lives—as opposed to ways

69

to fulfill our desires. We might lust after our desires, but we don't rely on them to live decently.

A new way to think about abundance might help us reframe the way we want to be in the world. What are some ways we can treat others more responsibly, more fairly, more respectfully? How might we treat Mother Earth more lovingly and justly?

One of the amazing things about living into an open-hearted definition of abundance is how wealthy being generous makes us feel.

# Initiate of Time

[Old age] is an intense and varied experience,
almost beyond our capacity at times, but something
to be carried high. If it is a long defeat it is also a
victory, meaningful for the initiates of time, if not
for those who have come less far.

— FLORIDA SCOTT-MAXWELL

Being older, especially as depicted in the current media, has
many negative connotations. Older people are often viewed
as physically, mentally, and even emotionally shut off—no
juice, not needed, indifferent to life. The media seems to focus
solely on the discomforts and limitations. The elderly are por-
trayed monolithically as people who can no longer drive,
have sex, think straight, walk, or hear.

But being older encompasses much more than the things
we can no longer do, or do in the same way. Eldering can be,
like every other stage of human development, vividly engaging and the opposite of boring—"an intense and varied experience" declares Scott-Maxwell. Growing older, like growing
into adulthood, entails challenges that are best met with curiosity and creativity. Remaining engaged with living, unafraid
of change, means conquering the negative stereotypes. Being

able to welcome change is a flag of victory to be "carried high."

For many of us, just the prospect of aging can loom like defeat. We carry all of our losses, large and small, into a battle we believe is lost before it starts. When we believe that we have no more loving, exploring, and discovering left to do, we have retreated before we've even tested our abilities. Becoming old can mean shutting down, but it doesn't have to.

If we instead bring our whole selves into the future, we may be newly baptized as "initiates of time" instead of its victims. How wonderful to live long enough to be inducted into the secrets of time! Only we can choose to see the years we live through as deserving of our passion and grace.

# Inside Outside

This is a delicious evening, when the whole body is
one sense, and imbibes delight through every pore.
I go and come with strange liberty.

—HENRY DAVID THOREAU

Hopefully, we've all experienced moments immersed in the
woods of our solitude. Some of us know early on how our
spirits need quiet to tap into the sources of our being, or the
source of all. Thoreau created his sanctuary at Walden Pond.
Others of us may come to this knowledge through chance,
still others through spiritual exploration.

If we immerse ourselves in the deep solitude and beauty
that nature offers, with trunks and leaves cushioning us from
extraneous sound and light, we can find the boundaries of
our being melt and a sense of oneness overtake us, our very
atoms shared with those of all that was, is, or will be.

Many religious traditions offer rituals and texts through
which we can find our quiet center. In nineteenth-century
New England, Thoreau's group of intellectuals were inspired
by Asian sacred writings. They interpreted them as showing
that anyone could experience the divine without the scaffolding of clergy and organized ritual. They shared the belief that

through communion with the natural world we enter sacred space.

How easy it can be to bring ourselves back to ourselves: we only have to make the time and find the will. Thoreau argued that we don't even need wilderness—though wild places often inspire us. He argued fervently that all we need can be seen and felt in our own backyards, through mindful observation of a tiny plant in seed, an ant going about its daily rounds, or a shoot poking itself sunward through the crevice of a rock.

As created beings, we can expand our awareness by exercising our "strange liberty" to know ourselves as one with the rest of the created world.

# The Life in What Is

I don't have much positive to say about motor
neuron disease. But it taught me not to pity myself,
because others were worse off and to get on with
what I still could do. I'm happier now than before
I developed the condition. I'm lucky to be working
in theoretical physics, one of the few areas in which
disability is not a serious handicap.

— STEPHEN HAWKING

It's counterintuitive, but time and again people who've suffered terrible illness tell of newfound happiness: having
wrestled with the ultimate fear, they find their spirits newly
centered. Indeed, the struggle with the fact of our mortality
has been a spiritual practice for millennia in Hinduism and
Tibetan Buddhism, among other traditions.

Stephen Hawking, who has suffered from Lou Gehrig's
disease for decades, is almost completely paralyzed. His story
is unique in that he has survived far longer than most victims
of the disease, and because he has continued to work at the
top of his profession for so long.

When someone who can only communicate painstakingly
through an elaborate computer system says he is happier than

he was before he fell ill, we have to pay attention. Even with Stephen Hawking's many resources, it's hard to imagine being *happier* when life is so circumscribed.

How could that be? The first thing Hawking says is that there are people who are much worse off. He has come to practice radical compassion. That takes spiritual discipline — constantly awakening one's heart to its connection to others.

Secondly, Hawking recognizes his good fortune in having work he loves that he can do in spite of his limitations. We all might benefit from thinking about what we could contribute, and how we'd continue connecting, if we were disabled in some way.

Think about your passion, about the ways you stay connected to the world and to others. Remember a time you were laid up — how did you continue to stay engaged, if at all? If your physical ability were to change, how might you continue to give of yourself?

# Sculpting a Life

> If only we knew
> as the carver knew.
>
> — David Whyte

Imagine, as this poet did, that you are having your portrait made, your face carved in beautiful wood. Not all of us would feel comfortable, especially as we grow older, with someone noticing our wrinkles and spots. At times we may fear that our faces will betray us, showing our soft spots and weak places.

What are those soft spots? We often worry about all the things on our to-do lists, things we've neglected or allowed to unravel. Things we still want to do but fear we won't get to. What remains undone in our relationships can be especially heavy baggage.

But if we trust in the force that created us—that force that knows us at our core and cherishes us the way an artist cherishes her creations—we may feel less afraid. If you've ever made anything, you know that mistakes can lead to new discoveries and unintended beauty. If you've ever carved, you know that the grain, the natural material you work with, is as fascinating as anything you could imagine.

Staying physically healthy as we grow older requires that we not burden ourselves with excess body weight—our bones and hearts don't need the extra pressure. The health of our spirits also requires a lighter load. We don't have to carry what we no longer need—old disappointments in ourselves, obsession with our flaws, or a nagging awareness of relationships we should mend or let go of. Taking the risk of revealing ourselves—boles, knots, and all—liberates more than our faces. It makes room for more meaningful concerns and deeper joys.

We were not made to be masks, lifeless and unmoving. The elder wisdom that we are not alone in our failings should bring a smile to our faces—we have nothing to hide or fear. Our fear of unmasking prevents us from knowing ourselves and those around us intimately and curiously, the way an artist gets to know her creation.

# The Open Ear

I waited patiently for the Lord;
he inclined to me and heard my cry.
He drew me up from the desolate pit,
out of the miry bog,
and set my feet upon a rock,
making my steps secure.

—PSALM 40

We don't need to know the details—we can fill in the blanks from our own hard times—but a whole chapter of a life is captured in this passage.

Who hasn't felt sunk in a desolate pit or miry bog? Who hasn't needed help escaping from the sticky mud of their worst thoughts, like revisiting the bad things they've done or had done to them? Who among us hasn't felt stuck in depression, anxiety, or addictive behavior?

We all know that patience and trust are vital to rising up from that pit and finding solid ground again. But when we are so low, these qualities can be hard to find. The psalmist's patience and trust come from a deep faith in a god who hears his pain, who "inclines to him," listening to his troubles.

For those of us who don't believe in such a god, it's hard not to envy those for whom God's imminent and saving presence is physically felt—a deity who *inclines, hears, draws,* and *sets,* mixing it up with us mortals. What if, in our despairing moments, we imagine an answering force? What if we let ourselves feel the gentle uplift and then relief of standing on the solid rock of hope? What if we didn't ask "who?" or "what?" but asked instead, "Why not?"

Looking ahead, we know that we might again find ourselves in a hopeless spot, again needing to be patient and to trust—in life, in love, or in the divine, whatever our bedrock beliefs. The psalm reminds us that we'll be raised from those depths and find ourselves grounded once again.

# Letting Be

It is usually best, when caring for the soul, to sit
with what is there and let your own imagination
move, instead of making empty wishes or attempt-
ing heroic changes.

— THOMAS MOORE

Most of us don't think much about where our innermost self
resides, but we've all felt disconnected from it sometimes.
Listening to music, doing yoga, or meditating are some of the
ways we can reconnect with our inner selves. Soulwork, some
might call it.

Many of us don't know what to make of the word *soul*,
preferring *ego* or *spirit* as words to describe the ineffable something we sense is our essence. It helps me to consider that *soul*
originally meant "from the sea," and to remember that our
distant forebears emerged from the waters to become bearers
of an animating essence, the presence beyond material we
call *soul*.

To be "from the sea" is to be fluid, generative, reflective,
and connected to all life. To care for the soul, therefore, means
doing what we can to develop and enhance these innate qualities. Sea creatures are fluid, following currents and using

what the wind and water provide to thrive. They don't try to change the winds or fight the waves. Moore, talking about our earliest relationships in families, suggests we do the same, using our imaginations to create a life that is full of loving relationships, regardless of our past.

Sea life glitters with gold and silver reflections. We creatures from the sea gleam still; when we allow ourselves to bask in the sunlight or moon glow long enough, we catch and throw back celestial glints. Being reflective also means being still, holding silence in our bodies so we can hear our hearts.

All life came from the sea and shares its chemistry in some way. Our very blood resembles sea water in its composition and in its flowing and ebbing. Caring for our sea-born souls means not wishing we were someone or something else—it means knowing ourselves to the core, even the scorpion fish and sharky parts. Consider how even these aspects might contribute to your soul's ecosystem, to your soul's health.

Scientists have discovered that the darkest, coldest—and also the hottest—parts of the ocean teem with new and unique life forms. Why should our deepest, least-visited depths be any different? And knowing how life feeds life, why not care for it all?

# A Second Life

I have enjoyed greatly the second blooming that
comes when you finish the life of the emotions and
of personal relations; and suddenly find—at the
age of fifty, say—that a whole new life has opened
before you, filled with things you can think about,
study, or read about. . . . It is as if a fresh sap of
ideas and thoughts was rising in you.

—AGATHA CHRISTIE

Comparing a human life to a tree's isn't unusual, but Christie's viewpoint is surprising. She hardly quit the "life of the
emotions and of personal relations" at age fifty: she was married to her second husband, she had a child and a grand-
child, she was active in various mystery writers' organizations
and made a Dame of the British Empire, and she continued
to write and sell the most popular plays and novels ever
written.

A "second blooming" is an experience shared by many in
middle age. While some of us focus on the new juices nourishing the life of the mind, others nurture a desire for social
contributions. Still others use their second wind to explore
spiritual and religious questions and practices.

Christie's description of a second life is reminiscent of the third stage in the ideal Hindu male's life—that of the *vanaprastha*, or hermit. Ideally, when a Hindu man has completed his duties as student and householder and done his bit for the community, he may renounce ordinary life and pleasures for a life of contemplation and retreat. He turns his attention toward the divine and, leaving life's suffering and corruptions behind, he prepares for the next life.

Christie likens our new focus later in life to sap. We may feel the woody juices rising, bringing new bloom to our being. Without the intense emotional demands of the early adult years, perhaps now with empty nests, we may find ourselves dormant and ready for a new season. The sap rises again, nourishing new growth.

# We Are All Pioneers Here

O God of life's venture, . . . we are thankful this
day for pioneers of the spirit . . . who took compassion into desolate places, and fed the hungry-
hearted with their love.

—A. POWELL DAVIES

We think of today's venture capitalists as bold and daring,
investing money, taking great financial risks. But it's only
money, and usually not even their own. The real venture is
life itself. Any night on the news, we can see the terrible risks
taken every day by thousands of people trying to farm tough
land, leaving their homelands in search of work, or protest-
ing for human rights.

To the spirit of life and love that inspires all those brave
enough to risk helping those in need, we owe our gratitude.
Without such a divine presence in our lives, how much harder
life would be. Many of those who are true venturers give of
themselves without much thought to the costs. They know
something much greater is at stake, and they are guided by
something much more wonderful than money. Their capital
is devotion, and because of their investment, we all stand to
reap huge dividends.

We find many reasons not to take such risks: we can't spend the time or the money, or afford the heartache. We hesitate to stick our necks out, uncertain what we're risking if we reach out.

But in the economy of compassion, what is the real cost to us? We start with simple actions. How much do we risk when we offer a smile and friendly word to a frazzled clerk at the store, to a distracted woman passing on the street, to a neighbor who keeps to himself? A smile costs us nothing, yet offers real nourishment. An open ear gives a 200-percent return on the investment of time. What stock does that? Then we might volunteer at a homeless shelter or nursing home, a soup kitchen or an ESL program. What are the real risks here?

It is not hard to recognize a person who is hungry-hearted. We only need to look in the mirror sometime when we feel forsaken. And when we look into the face of another, listen to their story, offer them a hot meal or a chance to work, we see the holy flame of our shared humanity. And that's beyond any price.

# Life Is But a Dream

Row, row, row your boat,
Gently down the stream.

—TRADITIONAL CHILDREN'S SONG

Most of us remember this childhood round. But it's funny how often as adults we need to re-learn the things we once knew by heart.

What we did—and do—know is that the song is reassuring. The task assigned us is clear and simple—to row our boats downstream. We're to row gently, with care for ourselves, for the oars and oarlocks, and for the boat. We go with, not against, the current that carries all boats, in time, to the sea; we do so with kind attention. Why? Because this existence is but a dream, or, as the Buddhist Diamond Sutra would put it, an illusion, a phantom.

The child's song seems simple and soothing, telling us to let go and go to sleep. But like a Buddhist teaching, it can also be taken as an exhortation to let go of material reality and float in the only true reality, which is this moment—and the next one, and the next one, which is now.

We have a hard time with letting go, because everyday life offers the comfort of affirming our physical being. The images in the Diamond Sutra describe this being as ephemera—a dew drop, a bubble, heat lightning, even the light from a cozy lamp. But fleeting light illuminates what we hold as real. Yes, we think, this is what makes life worth living—this world.

Then the blade of awareness falls—what felt so real proves illusory. An illusion is a trick, a falsehood. Dreams can be fearsome, terrifying, thrilling, puzzling, or delicious. But they aren't real, and don't serve as a solid basis for our priorities or values. What are we to make of this world?

When we are spiritually awake we understand we've been trying to grab a bubble, a fragile beauty called reality. To continue grasping after that only increases our suffering, and the suffering of others. When we accept that only the present moment is ours, we will row more merrily on this stream of life.

# Flashes of Fire

Set me as a seal upon your heart,
as a seal upon your arm;
for love is strong as death,
passion fierce as the grave.

—SONG OF SOLOMON 8:6

This most famous song describes a fiery love, using images from a faraway landscape that include sheep and goats, vines and lilies, towers and doves, rare perfumes and gazelles. We resonate with the purity of these ancient images, and we easily recognize the urgent desire of the cascading verses describing kisses and lovemaking—the sheer pleasure of embodied love, of joining our physical and emotional selves.

As we grow older, this kind of urgency can mellow somewhat, and our bodies may begin to change in ways that inspire us to be more creative than fiery in our lovemaking. Our bodies teach us about the effects of time, and we learn the rewards of tenderness and patience.

"To be set as seals"—think of molten crimson wax, firmly holding the shape of its stamp. Museums have seals that have outlasted the vellum they once kept private. A seal upon the heart of our lover declares that heart as exclusively ours. And a seal upon our lover's arm claims their body. Body and soul, we are one forever, passion proclaims.

Perhaps that is the role of passion—to burn bright and hot enough to melt the hard wax of self so our lover can make an enduring impression. The grave is fierce, after all, calling us all to our fate. When passion for another blazes, love may indeed be as strong as death.

# *Cornucopia*

Inner harvesting means that you actually begin to
sift the fruits of your experience. You begin to
group, select, and integrate them.

—JOHN O'DONOHUE

Farmers know that harvesting is intense work, requiring many
hands. They also know to celebrate a successful harvest with
feasting, music, and dance. Successfully harvesting our lives
requires sharing both effort and joy.

Picking, sorting, and then preserving the best fruits of our
lives for the first time can be a challenge. In the market, we
may know to tap a melon, sniff a pineapple, or heft an apple,
but we don't yet know how to choose ripe memories, experiences, and wisdom. So we ask long-time farmers, who know
each fruit ripens in its own time and can teach us how to tell
when the time has come.

Once we discern that an experience is ready to be plucked,
we may need some help—our inner harvest can sometimes
be too heavy or too messy for one person alone. Like any sen-
sible farmer, we get others to help bring in our crops—trusted
family, friends, clergy, spiritual directors, and if needed,
psychologists.

Once in, the crop must be sorted. Some of the fruits of our lives may be most delicious if squeezed for juice. Others may need to be preserved in some sweet or savory way for later use. Some may need to be shared and eaten right away to capture their truest essence. The fruits of our lives can nurture us if we transform them through writing, artwork, or mentoring; they can become sustaining to others if we use them to deepen our spiritual lives—making amends, acting for justice, or forgiving others, for example.

Of course, we should celebrate once this bounty is reaped. In Italy, there's a saying: "At the table, one never ages." To join with others in savoring the fruits of our experiences—our loves, our suffering, and our joy—that is to feast at a timeless table.

And when our cornucopia is full, we give thanks.

# On This Dust Mote

So the whole cosmos is a grain of rice.

— CHUANG TZU

Sometimes we get fed up with relativity. We want to know which it is—great or small, important or immaterial, lasting or not. We want to be told in certain terms what "reality" is. And sometimes we revel in playing with the mystery of it all: We live on a planet, a huge expanse of earth and ocean, yet know ourselves to be, as Carl Sagan put it, "inhabitants of a dust mote in a cosmos" that, for all we know, is in turn a mote in *its* cosmos.

Let's boggle our minds and sit with a rice grain for a moment. Imagine that, as the cosmos holds galaxies, stars, planets, and, yes, us, so a single grain holds infinite potential. It contains leaves and roots, flowers and pollen, and sheaves of more rice grains. And consider that each grain of pollen is inhabited by infinitely smaller beings. And within that grain of pollen lies the potential for thousands, even millions, more grains, and within those grains, again thousands and millions more. Maybe our universe is packed as tightly as a single rice grain.

Contemplating the infinite nature of the world can provide us with a new perspective on our lives. It can make us much less concerned about the make of our car or the neighbor's new swimming pool. It can be as calming as watching the mirrored clouds floating across a rice paddy.

Chuang Tzu, a Taoist writer, compares the tip of a hair to a mountain. Seen under a microscope, a hair's tip has crags and peaks, ridges and false summits. It's a regular Mount Everest from that point of view. It's amazing that, two thousand years before microscopes were invented, Chuang Tzu gave such thought to the trap of our perspective that he could provide such an insight. One of the wonders of being human is having an imagination that gives us access to new perspectives. Hope for greater wisdom lies in making the mental climb for a relative view.

# Falling in Love

Fall in love:
That is doing something!

— Sheikh Khwaja Abdullah Ansari

One funny thing about the term *falling in love* is that most of us, from infancy on, try *not* to fall. Learning to walk, run, ride a bike, or ski, we attend carefully to our balance, we fine-tune our coordination, and we learn to avoid wobbling.

But many of us desire nothing more, at certain times in our lives, than to fall head over keister into someone's heart, and vice versa. Our stomachs lurch and our brains get confused when we first fall in love, like they do when we tumble.

Spiritually, most of us try not to surrender our identity or freedom to something greater. We cling to familiar notions of selfhood and independence. We may try spiritual or religious practices, but find we are commitment phobic when it comes to sustaining or deepening our practice. We do almost anything to avoid giving up our familiar sense of control.

But if your spirit hungers, this may be the time to fall hard, fall head over heels into passionate commitment to something greater than another person. Fall for the sacred. Surrender to a passion for whatever is most holy to you. If you seek love, you must open up to love. If you fall head over the heels for the Ultimate, you'll find yourself feeding more than your own spirit.

# Slave No More

The miracle of Exodus is that a group of people
finally realized for themselves, for us, and for all
time that you cannot stay in Egypt.

—JOHN HAYS NICHOLS

We forget, when reading Exodus or hearing the story at a
seder, that the Jewish people were happy to follow Moses,
Aaron, and Miriam out of slavery—until they hit the desert.
They made the easiest mistake in the world—to forget that
deciding to make a change, to try for something better for
yourselves and your community, involves giving something
else up.

They had to do a lot of spiritual work. They wrestled with
doubt and faith, like everyone does during a time of change.
They missed knowing where their bread was coming from.
They did not want to trust that things would work out, and
they worried that their leaders were more lost than they were.

They had to learn to trust that God had their backs. It was
not an easy lesson. It never is. We are delivered by wise and
faithful people into a strange new land, and right away we
miss the familiar, small comforts. We engage in turf wars and
we start to worship golden things. We fail to recognize manna

when it falls right in front of us, and we forget to give thanks to the Spirit leading us to a new life.

Mostly, unless we find our inner Moses, we forget that our freedom is intertwined with that of those around us. We forget how important it is to have basic respect for others and for their searches for freedom. And we forget how miserable we were in our old lives, doing what we were forced to do by people who didn't respect us.

We stay in Egypt at the peril of our lives and our community's life. When we feel so trapped that we're willing to grab what we can carry and run like hell, we are ready for change, for new learning, and for a greater purpose than a day's worth of bread.

We can't stay in Egypt. Being slaves to the past, to a notion of security, to a state, kills our souls—and maybe our bodies, too.

# *What's New?*

Browning ground turkey while your children are
arguing in the kitchen, you may not feel connected
to this great mystery, but you are. This is the sort of
thing that parents, poets, mystics, and monks come
to know very well, if they are willing to be always
beginners, setting yesterday's burdens behind them
in order to recommit themselves to each new day.

—KATHLEEN NORRIS

At the day's end, on a bus or at the kitchen stove, all we dream
of is putting our feet up, turning on the TV, or opening the
newspaper. A martini would help, too. We think we'll be satisfied, at peace, if only we can tune out, and so we disconnect
from our surroundings, the people around us, our thoughts,
and even our feelings.

Too often we settle for boredom and call it peace. We fall,
as though off a log, into routines that come to resemble long,
forced marches more than joyful pilgrimages. When the start
of the day feels like picking up the burdens of our lives and
heaving them onto our backs to go another forty miles . . .
well, it's no wonder anti-depressant medication sells so well.

How can we face repeated but needed tasks each day? How do we survive a life governed by simple and seemingly redundant chores?

The answer is deceptively simple: Put aside the past and begin each day with beginner's eyes. Simple, yes, but it requires the energy, goodwill, and insatiable curiosity of a child. The eyes of a child are beginner's eyes. The Buddha, Jesus, and others taught that becoming more childlike leads to greater fulfillment.

Naturally, as we grow older, it feels harder to begin each day as if we were new at this living business. We tend to make shopping lists of goals and pile up dirty heaps of regret. Norris tells us that these are burdens best left behind if we want to recommit to living fully each day.

Each new day brings opportunities for heart-stopping wonder and simple contentment if we make time to awaken to our living.

# Out of Eden

If you remove the yoke from among you,
the pointing of the finger, the speaking of evil,
if you offer your food to the hungry
and satisfy the needs of the afflicted . . .
you shall be like a watered garden,
like a spring of water,
whose waters never fail.

—Isaiah 58:9–11

Have you ever watched oxen pulling a load? The mighty beasts, when yoked in teams, do the work of tens of men. The carved wooden whiffletrees that connect them are amazing tools; strong, yet not too heavy, they link and direct the animals' efforts.

Yokes were important and productive tools for civilization, but they have a shadow side as well. When we're yoked, we're chained to the goals of people with whom we might not agree. The slavery of conformity was decried by the prophet Isaiah because he felt that the Jewish people were becoming narrow-minded, selfish, and oppressive.

It's so easy to judge and exclude those who look different, who haven't got much money, or who aren't comfortable in social settings. When we yoke ourselves to a community whose values are mean spirited, we give up the freedom to open our hearts and think for ourselves.

The yokes we bear can serve either the common good or one group's narrow agenda. They can increase our strength when we pull with others or they can keep us from moving forward.

Because they don't know about things they haven't experienced, children don't understand the possibilities for community—whether it's marked by oppression or abundance for all. Young people watch and copy us. We must choose our yokes with care.

# The Confidence Game

Blocking is essentially an issue of faith. Rather than trust our intuition, our talent, our skill, our desire, we fear where our creator is taking us with this creativity.

— JULIA CAMERON

Have you ever felt stuck? Have you ever experienced that leaden door of "I can't" swing shut when you're trying to do something you love? Authors call it writer's block and Julia Cameron, an experienced artist, considers it to be a spiritual problem.

*Blocks* call to mind the boldly colored toys of our childhood. Those wooden cubes, each side decorated with a letter, helped us learn to spell our first words. Children use blocks to make real some fantasy or to follow whimsy. With a little imagination, all kinds of worlds are possible—castles, factories, homes, fire stations, futuristic cities. Blocks can be vehicles for expression, for shared vision, and fun.

Not the blocks of the creative spirit, however. These often come from lack of confidence in ourselves—fear and doubt that can wall us off from our expressing our truth, imagination, or joy. Such blocks prevent us from expressing a most human need—to make our meaning available to others.

A block, like any destructive force, takes many forms and can be difficult to spot at first. The main ingredient is "I can't." And the greatest source of "I can't" is our fear of being judged inadequate, of seeming foolish, of the unknown, or even of success.

When our creativity feels cut off or shut down, there are some ways to regain our perspective and trust once again in ourselves and the source of all life. These include meditating, taking long walks, praying, journaling, and playing. We might try finger painting, dancing, making music on the piano or with a comb and waxed paper—there are hundreds of ways to get back in touch with our open and inventive selves.

The wellsprings of our imagination may feel dry, but if we trust in the generative spirit, we'll be more willing to be guided by our own wisdom and passion—and find again our path to making meaning, and even art, of our experience.

# Besotted with Love

What drunkenness is this that brings me hope —
Who was the Cup-bearer, and whence the wine?

— HAFIZ

It's not surprising that, long ago, intoxication was integral to attaining insight into the sacred forces that governed our lives. The inebriation Hafiz seeks is the intoxicating experience of falling in love with the Ultimate, whom he also calls the Beloved.

Imagine that you and an unknowable cup-bearer enter a state of self-forgetful bliss. Imagine that this is our true purpose — that we are here because we are loved and our beloved asks only that we share this love.

In accepting that such bliss is our birthright, we find hope. Our being is enough; we are loved unconditionally. Even though we've made mistakes and been unloving, we can be transformed through the forgiveness of divine love into the lovable people we know ourselves to be.

When we are too insecure or busy, or too judgmental, we forget who our friends are. We lose hope that our humanity is enough, that we are enough, that we are beloved, in spite of letting others and ourselves down.

105

Where does this invitation to bliss come from? Who brings us the cup of Love? The Eternal, the Ultimate, God, or Goddess—we know this source of life by many names, or we may not know what to call her. The name doesn't matter—what matters is that we accept the gift.

# Forest Bathing

Some people like broadleaf forests and others prefer forests of conifer trees like hinoki cypress that
give off a strong aroma. I hope people try to find a
forest that suits their tastes and visit them [sic] from
time to time.

—YOSHIFUMI MIYAZAKI

Many of us know the sense of well-being a walk in the woods
can create in us. The Japanese, rooted in the Shinto reverence for nature, named this phenomenon *shinrinyoku*, or
"forest bathing."

The Japanese take bathing seriously. To defuse the stresses
of living in a densely populated, highly competitive society,
they have perfected the profoundly relaxing hot-soak approach
to bathing. Americans are shower people. We shower quickly,
often while listening to the traffic reports and news. We may
take pills to help us sleep and lower our blood pressure,
indulge in whatever to unwind, and get massages to relax our
muscles. When did we forget about the pleasures of soaking
our souls in the most soothing environments we can find?

When did we forgo a long walk outside in favor of pills
and services? We know the psychological benefits of being

outdoors—the smells, sights, sounds, and textures of nature washing over us calm our bodies and salve our spirits. We don't have to take our blood pressure to know that we feel more relaxed after a morning in the garden, twilight on a pond, or a leisurely afternoon among the trees.

The New England Transcendentalists were heavily influenced by Eastern religions' reverence for the natural world, and many of them found more spiritual solace outdoors than in houses of worship. In the hurly-burly of our daily lives, we too can cleanse our spirits by immersing ourselves— bathing, if you will—in the physical world, the world of growing, living, reproducing, and dying that is so present in the woods, or even in a local park.

Many of us have a favorite kind of tree. When we walk in the woods, we might head straight for the oak groves, with their leathery leaves that hang on and on all winter. Or we might retreat to some deep jungley fronds and vines. Some prefer the carpeted piney stands, with their warm, sharp scent. How might our week or month be different if we took more frequent dips in the out-of-doors? A weekly bath for the soul is a relaxing, old-fashioned way to clear the heart and mind and connect with that which is greater.

# An Unwrinkled Heart

To keep the heart unwrinkled, to be hopeful,
kindly, cheerful, reverent—that is to triumph over
old age.

— Thomas Bailey Aldrich

Watching our elders, we glimpse how hard the transitions of
aging can be and this Boy Scout pledge of an aphorism hardly
seems adequate to the challenges. Aldrich, a prolific, highly
regarded author and early editor of *The Atlantic Monthly*,
lived a long and successful life. Given his achievements, we
might imagine that he found it easier than most to stay "hopeful, kind, cheerful, and reverent."

But Aldrich experienced more than his share of disappointment and loss. His father died when he was in his teens. At
sixteen, he gave up his dream of college and travelled to New
York to work for his uncle. He is not remembered for writing
the book that inspired Mark Twain's *Huckleberry Finn*, even
though he did. He was blessed with twin boys, but one son
predeceased him, dying young of tuberculosis.

Even people born to a life of silver-spoons smack up against
sorrow. We're all vulnerable to what can grieve us, weary our
spirits, and burden us with pain. And the wear and tear of

109

living shrinks our hearts—*if* we allow it to. We can't stop the aging process, but by keeping our hearts nourished and well-exercised we can keep them youthful. This requires, first of all, our intention—adopting a spiritual practice to bolster our spirits. Second, we need a community, either small or large. Hopefulness, kindness, optimism, and wonderment are the benefits of a heart's daily workout. In a spiritually attuned community, we can find great personal trainers who offer understanding, advice, and encouragement when we're flagging. How better to keep our (older and wiser) hearts full and pumping than by using them well?

A daily workout of joy and wonder, compassion and gratitude keeps the heart muscle from withering.

# The Quilt of Day

Every day is a god, each day is a god, and holiness
holds forth in time. I worship each god, I praise
each day splintered down, splintered down and
wrapped in time like a husk, a husk of many colors
spreading, at dawn fast over the mountains split.
I wake in a god. I wake in arms holding my quilt,
holding me as best they can inside my quilt.

—ANNIE DILLARD

Why aren't we shattered awake more often? Why don't we
enter each day worshipping and praising the holy presence
that holds us? The simple act of waking up can evoke feelings
of awe and joy, if we consider the one-in-a-billion chances
of it, and remember all the blessings of being alive. The hol-
low husk of time holds each day, and each day holds all
that is worthy of our devotion—radiance, warmth, time itself
shifting and splitting into myriad possibilities. Each day offers
blessings, small and large moments of grace, accidents avoided,
disappointments that do not materialize. While husks of time
can't protect us from loss or betrayal, from disappointment or
misfortune, we are held nonetheless.

We cannot change the way things are, but we can change how we view what is—we can see the dawn, the peaks, and the splintered, splintering light as a quilt, as a god. We can grow to accept that each and every day holds us as best it can.

# A Home for Grief

Ah, grief, I should not treat you
like a homeless dog.

— DENISE LEVERTOV

Many of us don't like to think or talk about our deepest losses; we try to lock them out of our minds and hearts, hoping the memories and feelings will go away and leave us alone. But what would happen if we allowed grief to come close, to sidle around the door, scout the kitchen floor, even sit beside a favorite easy chair?

It's counterintuitive, this making room for grief. When we mourn, we are often encouraged to "get over it" and "get on with our lives." But as we've often seen, spiritual wisdom comes from doing the opposite of what our fight-or-flight mechanism tells us to do. The Buddha said that our harshest experiences are the best teachers of loving-kindness.

We can spend huge amounts of energy shooing away our most difficult feelings, ignoring their insistent whining. We can be torn between letting them in and calling the pound. Giving grief a little nurture is a new way to deal with loss. When we recognize our grief as a homeless, desperate dog, deserving of our compassion, we can adopt it and bring it into our hearts in a way that may be more helpful than repressing it. We open our hearts to an emotion that only craves a warm place to lie down, a little nourishment, and a pat now and again.

Perhaps we come to see how our grief needs us more than we need it to survive. In showing loving-kindness to our own mourning, we transform it. We give a needy, hungry spirit a home and it stops haunting us and comes to offer us comfort. Levertov's poem ends with recognition—the speaker comes to know grief as her "own dog" and herself as its proper companion.

In giving a proper place in our hearts to our homeless hurt, we gain more space for living and loving. By trusting grief enough to welcome it, our mourning brings us back into relationship with our whole selves.

# Being in Awe

After all, there's the longest speech you've given,
there's the most games you played, there's the
longest drive you've driven, and there's the best
catch you made. And although these white-ribbon
finishes aren't always surrounded by cheering
crowds, flashing cameras, and newspaper headlines,
the truth is that doesn't matter.

— Neil Pasricha

Sometimes you find wisdom in unexpected places. I stumbled
on Pasricha's blog, "1000 Awesome Things" by happy acci-
dent: He's been awed by the everyday on a daily basis for three
years and several books, and he shows no signs of letting up.

And I mean ordinary—this quote is about a father's pride
in his baby's longest burb ever. Other experiences he brings to
our attention and inspiration include things like the brocco-
flower, animal hangouts, times when your shampoo and con-
ditioner run out at the same time, and music loud enough to
get lost in.

We may strive and compete to set records that the world
will notice, but something gets lost in the effort—a whole lot
of everyday living, being, and delight. As part of that delight,

Pasricha would include personal achievement, and as we grow older, our sense of achievement may change. We might come to agree with the goals laid out in Bessie Anderson Stanley's popular definition of success: "He has achieved success who has lived well, laughed often, and loved much."

Pasricha gets it—each day does offer us a chance at wonderment and feeling blessed by ordinary miracles. He's right about outgrowing the need for cheering crowds, nice as they might be. Living is not about making headlines or the red carpet—it's about *being* in awe.

# Living Streams

Jesus said, "Become passers-by."

—GOSPEL OF THOMAS 42

This saying of Jesus from a long-lost Gnostic gospel carries such potency and mystery that it was carried on in the Islamic tradition. Its interpreters agree on one point: we are to achieve some kind of distance from the world.

But what kind of distance? Where does this idea put us in relationship to our families, our communities, and our culture? Should we not care? Should we become ascetics? Gypsies? Does following a spiritual path require us to renounce material things? Family ties? Our community?

Perhaps. In the canonical gospels, Jesus at times rejects his own family. He is skeptical of the ability of the wealthy to enter the kingdom of heaven. He wanders from place to place, and needs long periods of isolation for prayer and reflection.

On the other hand, Jesus also has intense relationships with his community of disciples, with several families, and with some of his own family members. He does not set up shop in any one place, and this feels empowering; spiritual awakenings can happen anywhere—at home, in the market-place, or on the street. They often occur when people gather

117

to share something, such as a prayer, a drink of water, a story, or grief. Epiphanies happen when feeding crowds, offering expensive ointments, in an orchard, or alone in a desert.

Jesus, like the prophet Muhammad, lived life deeply, but not so dug in that he clung to it. Thomas's advice to "become passers-by" calls us to the way of transience. Dipping your hand into a stream lets you feel its silken thrust or slake a momentary thirst, but trying to capture a stream is like trying to hold onto the material aspects of life. A captured stream becomes stagnant and even dangerous to drink from.

Being a passer-by is being a clear stream, a lively force—nurturing, catching all the available light, and carrying it forward.

# *Taking Stock*

In the middle of the journey of our life
I found myself astray in a dark wood.

— Dante Alighieri,
translated by Seamus Heaney

We are all on a journey. All great poems and parables, dramas and sagas, awaken us to this truth, but most of us don't think about our lives this way. Because this journey isn't one we get to make an itinerary for. Some of us aren't even sure who sold us the ticket.

Like Dorothy on her yellow brick road, we are faced with many choices along the way, and many get made for us. We know where the trip starts, and that there is usually a middle to it, and we also know where the path ends. The journey involves lots of questions and no clear answers. What would I be happiest doing? What other vocation calls to me? Will I or can I get married? Have kids? How will I care for my parents when they get too old to care for themselves? What will an empty nest feel like? How can I make the best use of the time I have left? How will I know when it's time to give up some independence? For some, these are the easy questions.

The questions grow more complex, and may take us from a straight path to a winding one and maybe to the dark, imponderable spiritual wilderness most questers find themselves in. How do I know what's right and what's wrong? How do I love myself even when I've made a bad choice? What should I do when I witness injustice? Am I being accountable to my best self? To the highest and best values? And what are those? How do I find my bearings again?

If you've ever found yourself in a truly deep forest, you know how it feels to be this lost. We're not talking about ordinary woods, but a vast tract, thick with brush and heavy boughs. There is a gloomy depth to thick woods that is unlike other darkness. Trodden paths, blazes, or cairns disappear, and we grow uneasy. We try to reason our way out, but we have no guidance. We grow disoriented, panic, and head blindly in one unpromising direction after another.

Poets say we need a guide. Historians tell us to consult the past. Some clergy might hand us a sacred text. But a native of the questions, a woodsperson, will tell us to sit down, take some calming breaths, clear a space, and light a fire. To find the way out, we figure out how we got in by retracing our steps or, better, climbing up high enough to get the larger picture. Then the way onward becomes clearer.

# We Rest

There is a love holding me.
There is a love holding you.
There is a love holding all.
We rest in that love.

— REBECCA PARKER

Simple, tough words to live by. And all the tougher if we don't feel held by anything, if we don't feel loved. What is "a love" anyway?

Suspend disbelief for a moment, assume this love exists, and ponder its attributes. It might feel like a palpable warmth, a feeling of soft strength enfolding you. Or it could be a sense that you are surrounded by and even filled with light.

Think of your favorite way of being held. Imagine that you are held that way this very moment. Find a peaceful place, somewhere you can gently speak to yourself out loud. Consider the text below a chant; chanting helps abstractions to enter the chambers of our hearts.

*I am held, and you are held, and all are held. Held in love, with love, by Love.*

Held not by obligation or guilt, but by love. When was the last time you noticed the embrace of the Universe? Imagine being held in huge, warm cradling hands. Imagine being held, not in the way of duty or greeting, but unconditionally and abidingly.

Sometimes it's impossible to feel lovable. How can there be a love so deep, so wide, so unending? Can it really embrace us, frail, torn, or unrepentant as we may feel?

*I am held, and you are held, and all are held. Held in love, with love, by Love.*

In our restless times, we find rest in this humming truth. Don't worry about anyone else. All are held in and by this love. Let distraction and worry go—you are loved and all are loved, period. Everyone and everything! Allow yourself to receive this embrace.

# Gotta Stand Up Before You Lie Down

> You may be thirty-eight years old, as I happen to
> be, and one day, some great opportunity stands
> before you and calls upon you to stand up for some
> great principle, some great issue, some great cause.
> And you refuse to do it because you are afraid. You
> refuse to do it because you want to live longer.
>
> — MARTIN LUTHER KING JR.

When was the last time you showed up to stand on the side of a position you believed in? When did you last write a letter to the editor, carry a sign, or march behind a banner you believed in? When did you last speak truth to power? One of the benefits of being older is that we know what it means to have people to support us when we've been treated unfairly, and we know how it feels to be wronged and alone. We also know what happens to our souls when we fail to stand on the side of love.

Fear leaves us vulnerable to killers of the spirit. Later in his speech, King reminds us that, though we may live to be ninety, if we don't at some time stand up for the right, the good, and the true, our spirit dies, even when our body breathes on.

Fear kills our minds and our spirits when it uses our own needs as an excuse not to defend basic respect and justice for all. It's hard. It takes strength of character and devotion to a high purpose to push aside such fear. King was able to do it because of the support of his family and friends, his community, and his allies. This love did not save him, but it did enable him to make a life so full of love that he left a legacy of equal rights and abiding hope to millions.

To be truly alive, we need to know what fear is holding our spirits down.

# Reclaiming Rest

> Sabbath honors the necessary wisdom of dormancy.
> If certain plant species, for example, do not lie
> dormant for winter, they will not bear fruit in the
> spring. If this continues for more than a season,
> the plant begins to die. If dormancy continues to
> be prevented, the entire species will die.
>
> — WAYNE MULLER

No wonder keeping the Sabbath, a day of rest for all, is one of the ten commandments Moses brought down to his people.

Dormancy isn't a concept contemporary Americans discuss much. The root of the word means sleep, which most American adults don't get enough of. It makes sense — we want to have it all but we can't shoehorn more hours into the day, so we steal them from our sleep. And studies show that we are stressed, depressed, and unproductive as a result. Muller's dire warning about a species deprived of its rest may apply to the human species as well.

A synonym for *dormant* is *fallow*. A friend recently used *fallow* to name what she worried others might view as laziness; she recognizes her own patterns of dormancy. *Fallow* implies fertility and fermentation. We need to reclaim this word, not just for our work lives, but for our spiritual well-being, and recover the Sabbath as time sacred to our fallowness.

Keeping the Sabbath day holy comes from Judaism. For Jews, Sabbath is a time for deep joy, for relaxing not just the body but the spirit, as it remembers the ease, peace, and holy oneness of the Garden of Eden. The Sabbath commandment reminds us to make a spiritual practice of resting, of sharing the earthly delights of meals, conversation, and walks with family and friends, and of being alone with our own thoughts, or with the Holy.

Allowing ourselves the blessing of dormancy, we center our lives again and allow the march of our days to become a divine saunter, a waltz, a nap.

# Iron Wheels

Now I am older, if not old, and I hate sorrow. I see
that it has no energy of its own, but uses mine,
furtively. I see that it is leaden, without breath,
and repetitious, and unsolvable.

— MARY OLIVER

For the young, intense emotions can seem glamorous. Before
we've seen much of life and the wildly different emotions it
can inspire, it's easy to become addicted to the drama and
mystery of passion, to be ruled by all our feelings, without
discernment.

But as we mature, we learn that some emotions are un-
healthy when we cling to them for too long. Sadness, the poet
says, is like pulling a great iron wheel to nowhere. Sorrow does
not heal, does not breathe on its own — its heaviness drags our
lives to near stopping. Pulling sorrow is work, but unlike creative effort, it saps all our vitality with no purpose or pleasure.

Yet, the temptation persists. What once glamorized us con-
tinues to enchant and enchain us. We continually risk letting
life happen to us instead of living it.

If we feel disconnected, caught in some spell, harnessed
to a dead weight, we can figure out what spell we've cast for

127

ourselves. Are we enchanted by a sensation that feels like living but is not? The hardest part is recognizing that we are enchanted. Less difficult is breaking the spell. According to ancient lore, an enchantment is not broken by a torrent of tears or brooding, but by a kiss. Love and connection are the way back to life.

# Recognition

When you wake up in the morning, tell yourself . . .
I have seen the beauty of good, and the ugliness of
evil, and have recognized that the wrongdoer has a
nature related to my own—not of the same blood
or birth, but the same mind, and possessing a share
of the divine.

—MARCUS AURELIUS

Barrel into your average morning and what happens? Too often
we find ourselves in a confrontation by ten o'clock and disillusioned with humanity by lunchtime. The variety of unpleas-
antness, mean-spiritedness, and evil our fellow humans are
capable of often shocks and sometimes sickens us. Our frus-
tration with others can fester and turn into anger. Pointing
fingers at the thoughtlessness and cruelty of others can blind
us to the truth about ourselves.

A Stoic philosopher, statesman, and emperor, Aurelius had
a front-row seat for the dramas of a mighty and complicated
civilization. As a young man, Aurelius trained as a priest and
became the leader of the sacred dance. But his leadership
skills thrust him from one kind of world into another, much

129

harsher one. He probably wrote his books of meditations during a campaign against people of the land known today as Hungary.

It's no surprise that Aurelius was a philosopher king. A warrior-dancer, he took stock of a lifetime of feelings—reverence, fondness, and jealousy—and concluded that we all hold the capacity for good and evil. Even so, he believed that we are vessels of a holy flame.

If you rebel at the idea of sharing anything with, say, a murderer, think about this question that Aurelius posed: Might we all be as ignorant of our divine nature as a murderer is? And is this one way in which we're all alike? Our hearts and minds can be as clouded by ignorance and fear as anyone else's.

When you wake to a new day, what word or gesture might remind you of your sacred connection to all humankind?

# Alone

I am way outside somewhere in the wilderness.
And it has been a long time of being in the wilderness. But I would be crazy if I didn't believe that
I deserve better, and that eventually it will come
out right.

— MAY SARTON

Throughout life we move back and forth between the poles
of community and individuality. Young children grow into
self-sufficiency as they mature but, if they're lucky, still trust
to loving hands to catch them when they fall. Later in life,
they may become part of that safety net for others as they
grow more capable. And as time goes on, most of us find ourselves again in need of loving hands to help us.

At any stage of life, spiritual maturity means being able to
enjoy the company of others while maintaining the ability
to sustain ourselves. Solitude gives us space to think our own
thoughts, pray our own prayers, and take measure of who
we have become. Most of us welcome solitude if we know we
have a caring community to rejoin when we're ready. But
when we feel misunderstood, undervalued, or marginalized,
solitude can be a confusing wilderness. When we don't choose

to be isolated, our aloneness bewilders us. We wonder or pray about why we are alone. Why now? Why here? What can be learned this time?

Sarton, a lesbian poet, found herself in a lonely wilderness at different times for different reasons. While she received some good reviews, she felt that none of the critics fairly assessed or recognized the full significance of her writings. She felt isolated from her peers and cast aside by critics.

Like Sarton, we'd worry about our sanity if we lost our belief in ourselves and our hope of rejoining a community. We have evolved as social beings who hunt and gather, dance and weave, flirt and worship together. Having faith in community and in our ability to nourish one another's purpose, courage, and hope is essential to our spiritual health. In cultivating this faith, we keep our balance and find our way out of the wilderness.

# Civilization and Generation

Civilization is the nurture of the child, its supportive
world, or it is nothing.

— KENNETH PATTON

*Civilization* is such a grand word, and we can stand up a
little straighter when we're reminded that we are part of such
a noble construct. The word may sound grand, but its meaning appears simple: the opposite of *barbarity*, or mindless cruelty, *civilization* means living under a system of civil law.

Pretty boring, we may think, until we ask: Why have a system at all? Why not let people just be themselves? If we
are honest with ourselves, we know that we are all capable of
angelic behavior and horrible devilry. We see it in a child's
development; unless they are encouraged to be civil, taught
to be careful with others, children can be hurtful and mean.
Left to our own untutored devices, we could create a cruel
and oppressive world.

Whether we have children or not, no one wants to live in
a *Lord of the Flies* world. We are the bearers of civilization,
carrying our wisdom about relationships and compassionate
communities from the past into the future.

133

By being honest with ourselves about what has nurtured the best in us, we can choose how to best cultivate the ground of our being, carrying the light to the next generation.

This is our most noble purpose, one we can feel proud to carry forward.

# *Crazy in Love*

I believe I should like to be a fool for love—for the
love of this world and of the beings that populate it.
A fool for the faith and trust I put in other people—
even though they have been known to let me
down—as many as six times before breakfast.

—DAVID KEYES

Nobody wants to feel like a fool. Most young people go to
great lengths to stifle their emerging personalities for fear of
seeming foolish.

But some fools are deliberate. They risk embarrassment
for the sake of something important—such as speaking truth
to power. In some classic literature, court jesters are the only
ones allowed to make fun of the king. These fools are willing
to be laughed at in order to be heard.

And then there are those who are willing to risk their hearts,
to put their faith in the goodness of others, knowing that the
world will call them fools for love if their trust is not vindicated.
Many people whose trust is broken decide to stop believing in
others. They become cynics to avoid feeling stupid again.

We will always be let down, just as we let others down—
though hopefully no more than three times before breakfast.

If we stop believing in the good faith and good intent of others, some part of us will be stunted. Without that trust, there is no space for us to develop intimacy. There's no room to forgive ourselves when we fail in loving, in being there for others. There's little room to embrace the world and to be embraced by it if we're always watching our backs.

Wise fools don't care about appearing slightly mad. Such fools assume others want what they want—truth, trust, forgiveness, and a crazy faith in the redemptive act of loving-kindness. It's far from foolish to want to work and play in such a world. In fact, it's the height of sanity.

# Betting on Futures

Our greatest responsibility is to be good ancestors.

— JONAS SALK

In middle age, few of us think of ourselves as ancestors. We all have them, of course, and occasionally think of those whose genes we carry. We may not often wonder how those who've gone before us considered their role in our lives. But Salk, the child of immigrant Jews, was very conscious of where and who he came from and of the risks his forebears took in order to ensure a better life for him.

Salk, of course, is remembered for creating a wildly successful vaccine against polio, a horrific disease that killed or maimed many. We may not remember the difficulty he encountered in establishing himself as a researcher because of quotas on Jewish people in academia and medicine. We may also forget his later work on AIDS research. Or his establishment of the Salk Institute for Biological Studies.

As we grow older and experience new perspectives on the generations, we can gain a greater sense of what matters most, and how to hold onto it and pass it on to those who come after us. Our responsibility is to our children's children or, if we do not have children of our own, to "the seventh generation," as the Iroquois put it.

It's hard to imagine seven generations into the future, but it is not at all hard to imagine what we'd want the children of that faraway time to have access to: health, shelter, education, and a spiritually sustaining community. As we grow older, it's heartening to think that we are much needed, especially to create that kind of future for all those people to come.

To be in relationship is to be responsive and responsible for that connection. What a spiritual adventure it is to hold in our hearts and our minds those who will walk this planet 140 years or more from now! That's the principle on which Salk shaped his life, and we too, in our own ways, can leave a rich legacy.

# An Altered State

What did you learn
from things you dropped and picked up

— JEANNE LOHMANN

These lines recall the gestures of knitting — dropped stitches picked up, making the chain of yarn whole again. But that elusive stitch might be dropped again, creating a hole instead of a whole. The entire process might teach us to accept failure as vital to becoming whole. We might try picking up a stitch we dropped in a friendship. Or we might mend a hole we left in our day's projects.

Dropping things can be the result of clumsiness, but we also drop what we've outgrown, what no longer works, or what has become habit. Maybe we were not careless but were listening to a deeper wisdom about what was needed to keep the knitting of our lives whole and the pattern evolving.

The image of a knitter carefully checking his work suggests a spiritual practice for the end of the day. We can take the time to contemplate where our soul is knitted together and where there are gaps. What got dropped? Does it matter?

If it's important to our wholeness—and the wholeness of the world—how do we pick up the lost stitches and weave them back into the fabric of our life?

Most importantly, holding that fabric loosely but with love, we can say, "I'm grateful for all I have learned today."

# Talk to the Wall

Rather than going after those walls and barriers with a sledgehammer, we pay close attention to them. With gentleness and honesty, we move closer to those walls. We touch them and smell them and get to know them well.

— PEMA CHÖDRÖN

Often the walls we've built around ourselves are constructed of fear, ignorance, and ego. If we build them without reflecting on why, we come to fear the walls themselves as they loom over us, shadowing our days.

Chödrön, a Buddhist nun, comes from a tradition that shuns violence, believing that aggression walls us off from the essence of being. Buddhism teaches us to approach what we hate or fear with a "beginner's eyes" and heart. What is the wall made of? How was it made? We can observe not only the wall but ourselves: How are we reacting to it? In what ways are we making it higher or thicker without meaning to? Since walls exist because we make them or accept them, we need to know their makers well in order to dismantle them permanently.

Taking a sledgehammer to a wall creates dust and shards of wood and plaster—in short, a huge mess. Instead, we could draw close to the wall and become familiar with it. What holds it up? How thick and sturdy is it really? Can we hear anything from the other side?

Once we know our walls intimately, we can begin to knock them down, give them less space in our heads and hearts. Our spirits might become softer and more open without all that harsh scaffolding. Walls that we weren't even aware we were building might be abandoned. And through the knowledge we gain, we may find ourselves free of a prison we built ourselves.

# So High, So Wide, So Deep

*Life's challenges are not supposed to paralyze you,
they're supposed to help you discover who you are.*

— BERNICE JOHNSON REAGON

We all know folks who have been laid low by setbacks, losses, and disabilities. We may have suffered from them ourselves, and felt our lives stall out. In those moments, we have no idea how long we will be stuck, weeks or months or years. It's not easy to see that there is still a brightness there, on the far horizon.

We can find that vantage point by digging through the rubble. In the aftermath of a natural disaster, one way survivors begin to put their lives back together is to search for what is still whole, useful, salvageable.

Another is through friends and strangers alike: I recently read about one family in New Jersey who lost everything in a flood, and the mother despaired most about losing the family photographs. A friend put out the all-call to everyone in the community and to far-flung family members. Before long, enough photos arrived to re-supply the images of that family's history, to restore the life-giving stories from the past so that they could move forward.

143

Some people find a new ground of being with the help of other people. Others find the freedom to learn and grow after they are stripped of the old husks of self. When poet Louise Gluck's house burned, destroying everything—including a manuscript that she'd been working on for a long time—she found, after the shock, a brand new way of being and new appreciation of non-attachment. Whether we regain our spiritual footing in community or individually, we can ground our spirit's growth in faith, in art, in nature, in reason, or, most often, a combination of all of them.

Aging poses its own set of challenges as our bodies slow down. The interesting question is not "How have you been laid flat by life?" It's "What did you learn about yourself when you rose to meet it?"

# *More*

... really, my mother
never knew about the world.

— EDWARD DORN

One of the gifts of maturity is the new perspective we gain on
our parents. As children, many of us regarded our parents as
forces of nature who were powerful, glamorous, necessary, or
just there. As we reach or exceed their ages, it's hard not to
think about the choices they made or that were thrust upon
them, and how their lives affected ours.

The speaker in this poem mourns his mother's lack of
awareness of the world outside her own domestic sphere. The
sad tone of the lines suggests a woman who had little interest
in her son's story as well, a son who grew up into a world she
didn't know.

But family life is a stew, and we need a long spoon to reach
into this matter of parents and children — of mothering and
fathering, and of growing up and going away. It's not easy to
know all about our parents, to sort through the ingredients
that made them act in certain ways, and engage in our lives
or with the world in other ways. Perhaps it was precisely his
mother's lack of awareness and curiosity that created in young

Edward a hunger for writing, which led him to explore new experiences.

Our families help shape us, but do not determine who we are. We find out who we are and what we are called to do in the world through creative acts, like making a poem, and through destructive ones, like tearing down old ideas and beliefs to gain fresh perspective. And we become our own selves when we are able to offer understanding and compassion to those who raised us.

# Leaving Home

Homesickness is a great teacher. It taught me, during an endless rainy fall, that I came from the arid lands, and liked where I came from. I was used to a dry clarity and sharpness in the air.

—Wallace Stegner

Perhaps you still long for that place that you consider home. You might not have lived there long—Stegner is remembering a home, a community, a land that his family lived in for only a handful of years. It was the first place where he felt rooted, the first place where he knew he belonged. Decades and many homes later, he writes, "At heart I was a nester, like my mother. I loved the place I was losing, the place that years of our lives had worn smooth."

He learned this about himself by following jobs that took him across the nation, to places where it rained a great deal, to cities, to places with great spreading trees and no horizon. By not being there, he learned where he felt held and where his vision was clear. Not all of us would feel at home in a sun-beaten, big sky place. Perhaps too much would be revealed; perhaps we'd feel too small under a vast dome of sky. Or maybe we'd miss the gentler sounds and sights of a moister climate.

Physically and emotionally, we do best when we have a place where we can retreat and renew ourselves. Ideally, we have a community—a religious or spiritual home where our spirit can rest. This helps us to stay centered in our values, in our daily practice, and in our desire to live loving and beloved lives.

But a place that is too comfortable can dull our growing. The bird's nest has long been for me a perfect image of home. Our spirits hatch beneath warm, nurturing wings, secure in a cozy nest. Once we are too big and feathered, we must learn to fly—through trial and error, practice, and necessity.

We can starve our spirits or leave them vulnerable to predators if we don't stretch our new wings and trust the wind to carry us to new heights, new places, and new awareness.

# Success

"I wish I could do more," my neighbor said, and all
I could think as I gazed at her, shining before me
in the electric air, was *What more need there be on
earth than this? Than you?*

—KATE BRAESTRUP

Hours into her widowhood, Braestrup recounts, her doorbell
was rung by a neighbor bearing a hot dish. In the face of the
young mother's enormous loss, the woman tearfully regretted
that a meal was all she brought. As life matures us and our
imaginations, we grow in compassion; when faced with the
inexplicable suffering life shows us, sometimes our feeling of
inadequacy grows too.

When we hear about another's loss, we move quickly from
"How awful!" to "How can I help?" Hearing about pain and
loss may hurl us back to a time when we suffered. To escape
what we fear might be a renewal of our pain, we hurry to be
doing, and forget about the simple power of being.

The neighbor gave thought to a young family's immedi-
ate needs and cooked a meal for them—she used her imagination and her courage. She showed up with her casserole
and her tears and her regret that she could not take away the

149

shock and pain or fix the huge hole just torn through another family. Showing up to share suffering takes empathy, selfless compassion, and yes, courage.

In the face of unbearable sorrow, to show up is 100 percent of the care we can give. It is a gift that spiritually mature people offer to one another, and it doesn't require words, or even casseroles. There is almost nothing we can say, but we can be present; we can bear loving witness to another's ache. And we can promise to walk with the person into the hope of a future beyond the devastation. Our presence in the face of the unbearable gives light to another's darkest hour. There is no gift more valuable.

# Universal Laws

When you're kind to people, and you pay attention, you make a field of comfort around them, and you get it back—the Golden Rule meets the Law of Karma meets Murphy's Law.

—ANNE LAMOTT

Annie Lamott, single mother of one son and a recovering alcoholic, describes the many ways in which her Christian faith has sustained her. She also welcomes wisdom from many sources, as we can see. Her perception of the collision—or collusion—of universal truths excites our imaginations because it brings them into uneasy but interesting dialogue. The ancient and venerable Golden Rule, which appears in many religious traditions, states that we should treat others as we would like to be treated.

The Law of Karma arose from ancient Indian religious beliefs. It states that there is a law of cause and effect in our energies and actions. That which we send forth returns to us one way or the other. Here we're pointed to a kind of justice operating in the world.

And then we can apply Murphy's Law, which may also come from ancient wisdom but was recycled decades ago as a modern factory management theory. It states that anything that can go wrong will. The point is to count on human error, not see it as the exception. Human fallibility, including our own, leads us right back to the need for a Golden Rule.

In order to prevent Murphy's Law from dictating the tenor of our relationships, our moods, or our approach to life, we need to make it second nature to treat everyone, including ourselves, with generous doses of kindness. And to reinforce this practice, the Karmic Law reminds us that we can only benefit from our kind and attentive treatment of others. Finally, we must accept that failure is part of what makes life interesting and provides us with opportunities to open our hearts and our minds.

# Sweet Slumber

You have put gladness in my heart
more than when their grain and wine abound.
I will both lie down and sleep in peace;
for you alone, O Lord, make me lie down in safety.

—Psalm 4:7–8

For much of our adult lives, many of us have been viewed as leaders, even if we are not actively heading a project or an institution. By virtue of being adults we are looked up to—as exemplars at work, for moral direction, or simply for having been around a long time. The importance and stress of our responsibilities may be obvious to others, or we may struggle in silence with obligations that are significant and difficult but underappreciated.

Tradition declares that David, warrior-priest-king of Israel, wrote these verses to be sung in the great temple, for all his people to hear and perhaps sing together. Other verses and other songs speak of enemies and attacks. This psalm answers the question "How do a king and a kingdom find peace?" How does anyone find peace in the face of the worries that come with making a life?

Whether or not he wrote it, we can relate to this song about the gladness in a leader's heart when his people reap a plentiful harvest and enjoy enough bread and wine. We have felt the contentment of seeing the bodies and hearts of those in our care nourished or known the anguish of not being able to provide enough.

As the spiritual leader of his people, David knows that the material harvest is not enough. To find the renewal he requires to keep on leading, he needs to "sleep in peace." Here he leads by proclaiming that only in giving our burdens over to God, to the Holy Mystery, can we find security and renewal.

This song reminds us that people can find rest, once they've done all they reasonably can, through trusting the Mystery. With the harvest safely in, we know to bow before the Mystery and open ourselves to the grace of self-forgetting sleep.

# Even After, Ever After

Even after the chemotherapy I said O you
Perfect roundness of celestial fruit.

—Patricia Goedicke

Bad stuff happens, and those whom we love to pieces are not shielded from it by our love. And that stinks worse than any skunk. Our journey through life teaches us, if it teaches us anything, to expect the unexpected. Some say that good things happen because of luck, merit, or grace. Others don't think about their good fortune much at all. But when something terrible overtakes us—a chronic illness or loss of work, for example—many of us are quick to blame our bad choices, bad people, or even our past sins.

When a loved one suffers, we do too. In our pain, we're often asked to make choices, to decide how to cope with a radically new situation that is beyond our control. Some of us, overwhelmed by a sense of responsibility or helplessness, may flee from it. That flight might take the form of denial or addictive behavior.

Goedicke chooses differently, writing later that she's "nuts about" her lover, showing us a different way to approach fear, a way that lifts us into laughter and delight. For aren't we all

155

in the end "celestial fruit," planted by a power we can only imagine? But is being head-over-heels in love a crazy response in the face of brutal mortality?

Crazy-mad love for another sure can seem nutty if you fear for their health or if their tragedy threatens to catch you in its net. Deep love can appear irrational if you're so tangled in your own ego that you cannot see your lover's face, drained by illness, as heavenly—if you cannot see that your lover's face is as perfect as eternity.

Faith is the act of living as if we are all nuts about each other. It makes the world a saner and more joyful place.

# Taking a Plunge

Perfection is nowhere,
she says, So stink.

— LISA COLT

Step up. Walk to the very end of the diving board. Revel in trial and error—how to hold arms, head, and neck, then push off with creaky knees and thighs, lifting then pointing your toes for ease of entry, and feel the clean knife-edge of water shooting along your torso as you enter the pool.

Such mastery and delight are not possible without first stinking like a rank beginner. We all know this with our heads, but that first step takes guts. To disrobe and walk the plank of learning—few of us have that courage naturally.

As we grow in experience, we do many things so well they seem effortless. The phrase "Perfection is nowhere" reminds us that the ideal exists only in our imagination, not in the real world. If we can only consider entering the water perfectly, then we will never take a dip.

If, all your life, you've watched others do difficult things beautifully and wanted to have their grace and courage, why not take the jump? Why not try to be the person you've dreamed you could be? What's the risk, to stink at it? Babies often stink, literally, at being people at first, but most grow up beautifully, with patient nurture, following the instinct to try something new, to live a dream.

There's a nakedness of the spirit that comes when we free ourselves from the fear of making a mistake. As adults, we're not often familiar with that kind of vulnerability. Spiritually mature people don't mind the falls, the smells, and the mess that go along with being beginners. They do know the perfect joy of trying and growing.

Why wait to dive into a new passion?

# Milk and Honey

The Lord said to him, "This is the land of which
I swore to Abraham, to Isaac, and to Jacob, saying,
'I will give it to your descendants'; I have let you
see it with your eyes, but you shall not cross over
there."

— DEUTERONOMY 34:4

The old song warns that the Jordan River, beyond which lies a land filled with everything we need, is chilly and cold. In the last chapter of the Torah, God tells Moses that he will not make that journey across—and will not live to see his people finally reach the land they left slavery to find.

God, being God, does not explain why such a faithful person isn't allowed to enjoy the promised land. We are not told why Moses, reportedly a vigorous 120-year-old, dies at that point. And as a final mystery, the site of the tomb of this faithful and courageous leader is oddly forgotten.

Numerous commentaries offer reasons, insights into God's wisdom, or scholarly speculation about this story. And we can wonder at the longevity of the patriarchs and their wives—to walk with God, it seems, is to live long and to thrive.

Moses did not start his life wishing to become God's prophet or the savior of his people. Like Siddhartha, he was raised to become a prince, and like the future Buddha, he opened his heart to a new set of values after he witnessed human suffering.

Moses fled the palace, and he fled from God's call. He stuttered, and at first refused to speak on God's behalf. But God is persistent, and so Moses, with his siblings, led the Jewish people on a forty-year trek toward freedom.

We can't always pursue our vision expecting to enjoy the rewards of our success. We might never reach our goal. But like Moses, we make the journey because it is the one we need to make to become our best selves—not for the fleeting good feeling of a red carpet walk, a gleaming trophy, or hoards of adoring fans.

Moses did not complain about God's decree. But he did mentor someone who could carry on, who would lead the people across that chilly, wide river into their future. Moses laid his hands on Joshua—an anointing and blessing gesture that filled Joshua "with the spirit of wisdom." And you can believe that, after forty years of building a community, moving it forward by demonstrating the benefits of a shared faith, Moses had a whole lot of wisdom to share.

Milk and honey are sweet and nourishing, but so is the knowledge that we've done all we can to see that others have what they need to reach their promised land.

# Belly Laughs

Laugh deep in the body,
Laugh down to your soul.

— JUDITH SORNBERGER

When I imagine a goddess, I imagine legs taller than tree trunks, arms big enough to embrace hills, a generous bosom, and a jiggly belly that jives when she laughs. I imagine that she loves to laugh, because I've caught her laughing at and with me sometimes. The Hindu elephant god Ganesh and the fat Buddha Budai are two more rotund, jolly spiritual beings. They confirm that cultivating our spiritual nature doesn't mean just being solemn. The Dalai Lama, for instance, often laughs during his public dharma talks and interviews.

As we grow older, many of us avoid thinking about our bellies because of the gravity tugging at our situations, so to speak. We all know that a smaller tummy is healthier. But for a moment, let's think symbolically about bellies, because, as the poet tells us, they can serve as doorways to our most sacred meeting places of body and soul.

Putting your hands on your belly and laughing, long and deeply, may feel a little goofy, but try it. Right now. And again.

The body needs no reason to laugh. Laughter swoops into the places where we know what we are—a holy house, a place where we meet the divine. For the Holy She, laughter is an invitation to be vulnerable, to be open to our divine natures. Letting our bellies roll with delight is the start of worth-ship—engaging in that which is most worthy.

Laugh for as long as you can one more time. What has changed? Are you smiling for no particular reason?

Why do we need a reason to laugh? Like the Buddha, or Ganesh, we can laugh simply to open the doors and windows of our souls, to acknowledge our delight with the world, to give to another the Spirit of Life, to invite in a big smiling goddess.

# Love Is All We Need

Jesus answered, "The first is 'Hear, O Israel: the Lord our God, the Lord is one; you shall love the Lord your God with all your heart, and with all your soul, and with all your mind, and with all your strength.' The second is this, 'You shall love your neighbor as yourself.' There is no other commandment greater than these."

—MARK 12:29–31

We can get so confused and even turned off by religious extremists who insist that, to be faithful or righteous or simply *right*, we must subscribe to a long list of doctrines and rules. Some religious traditions, though, take a different approach and keep it simple.

By simple, I do not mean simplistic. Jesus' quote from the Gospel According to Mark appears simple. In response to a trick question about which of the commandments was the most important, Jesus doesn't hesitate. He answers that the first commandment is to love God with everything we've got. He doesn't say "obey" or "fear," but "love"—with heart, mind, soul, and body. The whole self, no holds barred.

That sounds like an obvious and even easy thing to do, but if we think about it, it's complex and messy. We *will* make mistakes, and we *will* stumble over our egos, and we *will* forget—all the human stuff that makes love worthwhile and hard. Love's not for wimps.

So the second important thing for faithful people to do is to love our neighbors—whatever that means—the same way we love ourselves. If we think this means our neighbors in the conventional sense of the term, we can get overwhelmed very quickly. Give as much thought and compassion to our next-door neighbors as we give to ourselves? Wherever we spend time, we have neighbors, so does this mean everyone everywhere? Jesus, committed to bringing more mercy and compassion to the practice of his faith, answered these questions through his parables and actions, offering everyone mercy and compassion.

French theologian Simone Weil offers a way to think about following this commandment. She writes, "The love of our neighbor in all its fullness simply means being able to say, *'What are you going through?'* " It's that simple, yet how hard it is to make the time to still our minds and ask that question of ourselves, much less of others—and then listen to the answer.

How is it with you? How is it with your spirit today?

# Seeker

You go to the desert.
You think of sand.

— MARGARET ATWOOD

For those of us seeking a transforming vision, the advice to imagine sand might be discouraging. We tend to imagine the divine as awesome and life changing. What is there to inspire such a vision in dunes?

Let's suspend all judgment, all expectation, all our skeptical notions for a little while. Let's stretch ourselves. Let's follow the ancient wisdom of desert fathers and mothers.

Picture a landscape of sand. See dawn's pink light caught on its unending hills. Watch white hot light beat across waves of dunes as time ticks by. In the bronze clarity of the setting sun, see fading light caught in rivulets of sand. Then, in the darkest hours, watch as the desert swallows all light but the stars.

Beautiful, you might exclaim at first. Vast, you would later declare. Monotonous, you might mutter after the first two days. After a week, you might be desperate to climb on a camel and hightail it out of there. You might think, "How ridiculous to imagine I could see the holy anywhere, much less in a pile of rock and mineral grains!"

The wise desert fathers and mothers say, "Keep looking— don't give up. To see the divine takes more than mere time."

Pick up a fistful of sand and hold it up to the light. Drop all but a few grains and look carefully. If you could magnify them, you'd see each as a tiny world. Imagine looking deep inside of one and seeing the atoms, each with its own energy and orbiting bodies. Now look up quickly—see the vastness of sand spread out to every horizon.

Within our sight is nothing, and everything.

# You Don't Need to Know

Kindly, the universe puts its great lips to my ear
and whispers, listen. Listen. You do not need to
know the name of god, or call it. You need only to
know that you do not know, and lift your face and
stand in its presence and give thanks.

— ELIZABETH TARBOX

This writer hears voices. She listens carefully. She urges us
to do the same. Can we hear a voice so tender amid all the
static of our lives? And how often in this world do we *not* need
to know something? Isn't there a fill-in-the-blank or yes/no
answer here?

We are so used to labeling, naming, categorizing, and filing
information. It's unsettling to hear that none of it matters if we
seek spiritual transcendence. But admitting we don't know
is the beginning of wisdom. Listening—literal or figurative—
is the doorway to truth.

Listening, however, is not always easy. Sitting quietly,
intent on catching not just the words of another, but all that
flows below the words, through the eyes or gestures. Or the
silences. This kind of listening takes intention and practice.

Tarbox offers her experience of listening to the Holy—and it is not different from actively listening to another person. Let go of ego, of the desire to know, and open ourselves to possibility and grace. And being thankful is key—this bringing of gratitude to our listening.

To start, all we need to do is admit ignorance. And then raise our faces in greeting, rest in the presence of the unknown, and speak our gratitude. That is enough.

# *Breath*

We build on foundations we did not lay. We warm
ourselves at fires we did not light. We sit in the
shade of trees we did not plant. We drink from
wells we did not dig. We profit from persons we
did not know. We are ever bound in community.

— PETER RAIBLE

Most of us know at least a little about the people whose eyes,
noses, or personalities we inherited. We may be lucky enough
to know that Great Uncle Bill had our same sly humor, or
Granny Hettie had a way with plants just like us. We gain
an appreciation of those who came before, and all they lived
through, when our elders tell stories about where we came
from and why. Prompted by a lovingly stored brooch or a carefully preserved military jacket, we also gain humility, for we
learn that we didn't invent bravery, generosity, or hard work.

Knowing about our ancestors connects us to them, to those
whose dreams and hopes brought us into being, who brought
those we love into being, whose loves and hates and choices
echo down through the ages, often guiding us.

And what about the dead we've never heard of, and all
those whom we've never met? We enjoy homes, parks, and

orchards made by people whose names are unknown to us. We benefit from reservoirs of water and of knowledge built by men and women long dead. And from long-ago astronomers and bakers, the first knitters and bricklayers.

How fortunate we are to stand on the shoulders of our ancestors and see a distant horizon. How much farther will future children's children see because of our effort and imagination?

# Pause, Traveler

it will take all your heart, it will take all your breath
it will be short, it will not be simple

—ADRIENNE RICH

For some, the lines above may sound a note of despair—
What do you mean "short"? I'm just getting traction here!
Are you saying this journey will be hard *and* brief?

Not so long ago, urban Europeans often spent Sunday
afternoons visiting catacombs—public places, often under-
ground, where the bones of the dead were displayed to make
room in the above-ground cemeteries. We might find the
idea morbid or depressing today. Yet in the catacombs below
the streets of Paris, wisdom sayings are posted in Latin and
Greek to inspire visitors to pause in their busy lives and think
about death.

"This is how it ends for us all—rich and poor alike—so
pause and take measure," the ancient and knowing voices
say. Others encourage us to make the best use of our days: to
spend our hearts and our breath and our minds doing good,
making each moment come alive. These dead urge us to put
aside needless worry, and stop numbing ourselves with denial
about where we are going.

Life is not simple for anyone. The old catacombs, however, show that our final stop on the earthly road is very simple and shared by all. The carefully arranged femurs and skulls spell messages for the living: Stay open to the opportunity that is your life, the chance to give and receive joy, and walk through the hard parts together.

Pause, traveler, the bones say, and do not waste another moment of the most valuable gift you will ever receive.

# What Waits for You

The central point of the world is the point where stillness and movement are together. Movement is time, but stillness is eternity. Realizing how this moment of your life is actually a moment of eternity, and experiencing the eternal aspect of what you're doing in the temporal experience—this is the mythological experience.

—JOSEPH CAMPBELL

As we grow older, many of us begin to appreciate how the very best parts of life vibrate in the intersection of stillness and movement. But what is this stillness, and what kind of movement makes for a satisfying life? What does it take to lift our being into the eternal now?

Campbell contends that religion in its storytelling form, in myths, provides the answer—which many of us know in our cores but not always in our conscious minds. In order to find the eternal in the now, we must take a heroic journey inward. And the great faiths say that journey is the most terrifying and exhilarating trip we'll ever take, but it's the only one that makes life worth living.

We have to go inward; we have to peel away our superficial layers to find what lies at our core—our passions, weaknesses, dreams, and goodness. And at the same time, we have to travel outward, staying open to whatever learning the world offers, whether through nature, other people, or other forms of life. Even imaginary beings, like the images from our dreams, can help us find out what we are meant to be, where we can find our bliss. In an interview with Bill Moyers, Campbell says, "If you do follow your bliss you put yourself on a kind of track that has been there all the while, waiting for you, and the life that you ought to be living is the one you are living."

There is no better time than the present to inhabit our bliss, here in the eternal now. No better time to begin the trip we may have put off for so many reasons—or to begin a new journey to the center of our being. No better time to follow our bliss, that state of being that all faiths point us toward. This is not the bliss of self-forgetting, but the bliss of finding ourselves and our place in the cosmos.

Growing is always rich with challenges and heartache, with dreams met and unmet. Always new dreams may be dreamed, and new challenges encountered. But if we live with the faith that we were meant to inhabit the eternal now, we will meet the challenges and find worthy dreams our whole life long.

Blessed be.